Silence Your Inner Critic

SILENCE YOUR INNER CRITIC

A Practical Guide to Building
a Positive Self-Relationship

AMBER MIKESELL

NEW YORK

LONDON • NASHVILLE • MELBOURNE • VANCOUVER

Silence Your Inner Critic

A Practical Guide to Building a Positive Self-Relationship

Published in New York, New York, by Morgan James Publishing. Morgan James is a trademark of Morgan James, LLC. www.MorganJamesPublishing.com

Proudly distributed by Publishers Group West®

A FREE ebook edition is available for you or a friend with the purchase of this print book.

CLEARLY SIGN YOUR NAME ABOVE

Instructions to claim your free ebook edition:
1. Visit MorganJamesBOGO.com
2. Sign your name CLEARLY in the space above
3. Complete the form and submit a photo of this entire page
4. You or your friend can download the ebook to your preferred device

ISBN 9781636985541 paperback
ISBN 9781636985558 ebook
ISBN 9781636985688 hardcover
Library of Congress Control Number:
2024943459

Cover Design by:
Chris Treccani
www.3dogcreative.net

Assisted by Austin Uhl

Images licensed through
Artist Leremy Gan

Morgan James is a proud partner of Habitat for Humanity Peninsula and Greater Williamsburg. Partners in building since 2006.

Get involved today! Visit: www.morgan-james-publishing.com/giving-back

To Jimmy and Alison, your light shines on eternally.

CONTENTS

INTRODUCTION 1

1. Born from the Shadows 3
The Origin of the Villainous Inner Critic. 3
The Rise of Your Inner Champion 4
The Call to Battle 6
Exploring the Shadow Cast During Your Youth 7
The Echoes of Societal Influences 10
The Veil of Tradition: The Inner Critic's Cultural Armor 12
Facing Down Your Inner Foes 13
In the Grip of Self-Limiting Beliefs 15
Battling the Inner Critic's External Voices 16
Level 1 Superhero Training: And So It Begins 18
Confronting the Forgotten Foes of Your Youth. 19
The Impact of Societal Forces 19
Unraveling the Inner Critic's Cultural Crusade 20
The Siege of the Self 20

2. The Hero's Trial 21
The Stealthy Siege on Your Self-Esteem 21
The Power to Shape Reality 22

The Crucible of Critique 24
The Prison of Self-Imposed Standards 25
The Treacherous Terrain of Self-Critique 26
Crossroads of Destiny: The Hero's Dilemma 28
Frayed Alliances. 29
Level 2 Superhero Training: Heroism Rising 31
   Darkness Falls Over Your Fortress of Confidence. 31
   Shaping Your Reality 31
   Fortress of Solitude: The Inner Critic's Barrier to Connection . . 31

3. Gearing up for the Quest. 33
The Hero's Essentials 33
   Tool #1: Mirror Technique. 34
   Tool #2: The Power of Thank You 37
   Tool #3: Challenge Your Inner Critics Narratives. 39
   Tool #4: Embrace the Learning Journey. 40
   Tool #5: Flip the Script 42
   The Hero's Essentials Summary 44
Level 3 Superhero Training: Quest Proficiency. 47
   The Fitness Journey Fumble 47
   The Relationship Rift. 47
   The Power to Say No 47

4. Exploring the Depths of Self 49
Illuminating Your Inner Realm 49
Mapping the Villain's Footsteps 50
Cultivating Nonjudgment 51
Challenging Negative Thought Patterns. 52
Embracing the Needs of the Inner Hero 54
Developing Mind-Reading Superpowers 56
The Superpower Trio 57
Level 4 Superhero Training: The First Adventure 58
   Entering the Labyrinth of Echoes 59

5. The Superpower Trio in Action 61

Inquiry of the Inner Hero 61

Self-Awareness Questions (SAQs) 62

Heart of a Hero: Training for Emotional Mastery 63

Feedback in the Superhero's Quest....................... 66

Superpower of Mindful Self-Observation................. 69

Unveiling Your Inner Dynamics........................ 71

Soul's Journey Tracking Sheet 72

Transforming Negative Self-Talk 74

Demystifying Mind Mirages 74

The Super Skill of Transformation..................... 76

Positive Affirmations List 77

Equipping Your Inner Champion 77

Level 5 Superhero Training: Using Your Arsenal........... 78

Dismantling the Myth: "Success Is Beyond My Reach"....... 78

Changing the "I Can't Change" Paradox 79

Unlearning the "I Can't Learn New Things" Lie 79

6. Your Battle Armor.......................... 81

The Three-Step Transformation 82

Vanquishing the Villain's Sidekicks 83

Speak to Yourself with Love and Kindness 83

Meditate and Explore Your Inner Landscape 85

The Voyage Within: A Meditation for Self-Discovery. 87

The Path to Redemption: A Meditation of Self-Forgiveness 90

Level 6 Superhero Training: Armor On 94

Navigating Personal Conflict 94

Overcoming a Setback 94

The Work Presentation Challenge 94

7. The Showdown Begins....................... 95

Unleash Your Authentic Hero 95

Developing Resilience in the Face of Judgment 96

Moving Beyond the Villain's Storyline 98
Escaping Your Inner Prison 100
Tablet of Internal Power 101
Level 7 Superhero Training: The Great Escape 102
The Unexpected Critique 102
The Crossroads of Life 102
The Sharing Paradigm 102

8. Self-Care for Superheroes 105
The Voyage to Self-Care Starts Here. 106
Fortifying Your Physical Fortress 107
Physical Self-Care Strategies 108
Bolstering Your Mental Powers 109
Blueprint for Building Mental Resilience 110
The Hero's Safeguard: Emotional Self-Care 111
Strengthening Your Emotional Resilience 112
Empowering Your Spirit 113
Building Your Spiritual Sanctum Sanctorum 114
The Never-Ending Battle 115
Level 8 Superhero Training: Power Up 116
The Dawn Patrol: Physical Self-Care 116
The Puzzle Box: Mental Self-Care 116
The Emotional Compass: Emotional Self-Care 117
The Soul Shield: Spiritual Self-Care 117

9. Boundary Lines Are Drawn 119
Creating an Impenetrable Force Field 120
Being a Superhero Is Not One-Sided 121
Setting Your Boundaries and Principles 121
Deciphering Your Hero's Code 122
Boundaries Unleashed: Crafting Your Hero's Code 124
Scribing the Principles of Your Inner Hero 126
Mobilizing Your Heroic Code 127

Defending Your Heroic Limits: Identifying and Countering
     Boundary Breaches 128
 Signs of Boundary Violations 128
 Tactics for Boundary Reinforcement 130
The Power of Positive Communication 131
Navigating Boundaries in the Relationship Maze 133
Level 9 Superhero Training: Mighty Deflection 134
 The Villain's Monologue 134
 The Boundary Simulation 134
 The Guiding Principles Manifesto 135

10. A Life of Triumph **137**
Life after You've Silenced Your Inner Critic 137
Sweeping the Streets of Your Inner Metropolis 137
Level 10 Superhero Training: Inner City Watch 139
 Heroic Reflections 140
 Empathy Patrol 140
 Journal of Justice 140
 Nature's Ally 140
 Kindhearted Acts of Care 140

11. Hero's Quest for Knowledge **141**
The Valor of Continuous Learning 142
 Key Benefits of Embracing Continuous Learning 142
Valiant Goals for Lifelong Learning 143
Level 11 Superhero Training: Lifelong Learning 144
 The Curiosity Crusade 145
 Empathy Encounter 145
 Mindful Mentorship 145
 Adversity Simulator 146
 Vision Quest 146

12. Our Journey Comes to an End **147**

Ten Treasures in Your Arsenal 147
Embarking on Your Superhero's Journey 148
Level 12 Superhero Training: A Hero's Life 150
Courageous Compassion Conclaves 150
Resilience Rallies 150
Learning League 151
True Self Check-Ins **151**

**CONCLUSION: Your Hero's Journey Continues
with Additional Tools........................... 153**
Top 10 Questions to Ask When Interviewing Your
                "Person in the Chair" (Your Coach) 153
Emotional Mind Map 156
Self-Care Routine Template......................... 156
Guided Meditations 157

ACKNOWLEDGMENTS 159
FINAL CALL TO ACTION 161
ABOUT THE AUTHOR......................... 163

INTRODUCTION

In every corner of the world, there exists an extraordinary universe—a realm where an epic superhero and a treacherous villain clash in a timeless battle for supremacy. While this epic tale could fill the pages of an entire comic book series, this is a battle that rages on within every one of us. It's the saga of the heroic "Inner Champion" versus the villainous "Inner Critic," and it consistently unleashes its chaos on the mindscape of humankind.

The superhero in this story, your Inner Champion, is your personal guardian. Endowed with the virtues of courage, resilience, and unyielding hope, it's the voice that calls you to greatness, that urges you to stand tall in the face of adversity and to leap toward your dreams with the confidence of the valiant heroes you've admired from afar. In its light, you find your strength, your passion, and the unbreakable will to succeed against all odds.

But lurking in the shadows, ever-present, is the formidable Inner Critic. A supervillain as old as time, the Inner Critic crafts illusions of doubt, fear, and limitation. With whispers that sound like truth, it seeks to darken your path, steal your joy, and vanquish your Inner Champion before you can even begin your hero's journey.

What if the key to unleashing your true potential, to become not simply the hero of your own story but the superhero within it, lies not in vanquishing this nefarious foe but in understanding it? Legendary superheroes find that their greatest growth springs from the ashes of their greatest battles, with each confrontation serving to forge them into stronger, more resilient champions.

This book is your invitation to grab your cape and embrace your journey of connecting with the superhero within. It is a guide through the thrilling highs and daunting lows of battling your Inner Critic.

Armed with the tools, strategies, and insights needed to empower your Inner Champion, you'll gain the superpowers necessary to silence your villainous foe and grow from each encounter. Through a mix of personal anecdotes, victorious tales from those who've walked this path, and an arsenal of transformative techniques, you will learn to navigate this epic adventure and rise into your unique superpowers.

This is more than a journey; it's your grand saga of facing down the darkness, rising with strength unimagined, and claiming your place among the legends.

Welcome to the rise of your Inner Champion.

1. BORN FROM THE SHADOWS

A master of disguise, your Inner Critic uses its super-powers to weave together your worst fears. This shape-shifting supervillain has become a seasoned storyteller, able to entice you with its lies as it traps you in darkness. The Inner Critic's power isn't in its physical might but exists in its ability to infiltrate your thoughts and beliefs, casting long shadows over your brightest aspirations and purest intentions.

THE ORIGIN OF THE VILLAINOUS INNER CRITIC

The Inner Critic is born out of the very fabric of your deepest fears, making it a foe that knows your most vulnerable points, giving it the ability to attack with precision. It builds walls around your hopes and dreams, brick by brick, with mortar made of "what ifs," "should haves," and "I'm not good enoughs." This supervillain strikes in those moments of hesitation, self-doubt, and self-comparison, turning each of them into hours of inaction and days of regret.

But there is hope! As formidable as this adversary is, it does have its weaknesses. For the Inner Critic to keep you in darkness and feed its superpowers, you must believe its stories.

As it whispers its fiction, you can engage the superpowers of your Inner Champion to counteract the false narratives, refusing to allow your Inner Critic to set your limitations, and turn down the role of victim or villain.

As much as we all desire to avoid the conflict between our Inner Champion and Inner Critic, there is a fundamental purpose for its existence. It challenges your Inner Champion, not out of malice but out of a form of necessity, pushing your inner superhero to question, to strive, and, ultimately, to rise. Battles with the Inner Critic are not just confrontations; they are superhero training, each one teaching your Inner Champion about the depths of your strength and the boundless potential of your spirit.

This means that as villainous as the Inner Critic may be, it's not an enemy to be defeated in a final, epic battle. It's an adversary to be understood, respected, and transcended. Its presence reminds our Inner Champion that growth comes through challenge, that light is most appreciated in the contrast of darkness, and that true victory lies in the ability to listen to the whispers of doubt without being swayed by them.

When you look at your journey in this way, your Inner Critic becomes a complex character, a necessary foe to your Inner Champion in the story *you* choose to write for your life. It's through this dynamic interaction, this interplay of doubt and belief, fear and courage, that the most profound transformations are accomplished. Your Inner Critic will remain formidable, but you realize it's not invincible. It becomes a catalyst for the rise of your truest self, pushing you toward a journey of endless self-knowing.

THE RISE OF YOUR INNER CHAMPION

In the heart of every individual, amid the cacophony of daily life and the whispers of self-doubt, resides an unsung hero: the Inner

Champion. This valiant hero is the essence of your potential, and it's often overlooked and underestimated among the shadows cast by your Inner Critic. Given the opportunity, this hero will rise and guide you through difficult times.

The Inner Champion possesses qualities not of physical strength or supernatural powers but of resilience, courage, and unyielding belief in your worth. These are true superpowers, latent within each of us, waiting for the spark of realization to ignite them into action. The Inner Champion sees the world not as a battlefield of limitations, but as an arena of limitless possibilities and a playground for your soul.

Initially, this hero within you might seem dormant, overshadowed by the looming figure of the Inner Critic. This villain, with its sidekicks of doubt and fear, crafts illusions designed to keep the Inner Champion in check, whispering tales of past failures and mirages of future disappointments. It's in this narrative, however, that your inner hero finds its purpose. As superheroes step into their authentic power, they come to understand that, without darkness, there can be no understanding of light; without challenge, there can be no growth.

The journey of the Inner Champion begins at this moment of realization—understanding that the voice of the Inner Critic, though loud, does not dictate truth. It's in this pivotal moment that your Inner Champion discovers its first superpower: **Awareness.** With awareness comes the ability to discern between the noise of criticism and the melody of potential.

Empowered by this newfound clarity, the Inner Champion learns to harness other superpowers, such as **Resilience**, the ability to rise from the ashes of failure; **Empathy**, the strength to offer compassion to oneself and others; and **Creativity**, the capability to envision solutions where the Inner Critic sees dead ends. These powers do not come from an external source, but from the deep wells of the human spirit, refined through trials and tribulations.

Victory for the Inner Champion isn't in the defeat of the Inner Critic, it's in the mastery of how to listen to its voice and know when to silence it. Each confrontation, each moment of doubt, becomes an opportunity for the Inner Champion to grow stronger, to refine its superpowers, and to rise higher. The presence of the Inner Critic, much like the supervillains in your favorite comics and movies, pushes your Inner Champion beyond its limits, forging a path of continuous growth and self-discovery.

As your Inner Champion emerges from the shadow of this supervillain giant, it stands as a beacon for others to see. It teaches us that the true measure of a hero is not in the battles won, but in the journey undertaken—the countless times we choose to rise, to listen to the voice of potential over doubt, and to embrace our inner power.

The rise of your Inner Champion is not simply a tale of an epic battle but is a journey of building a positive self-relationship. It's a narrative each of us can live, where your Inner Champion, once underestimated, shines as the true superhero of your story, illuminating the path to your greatest potential.

THE CALL TO BATTLE

When you think about the heroes of your life, I would venture to say that each was likely forged from the fires of their life challenges. They weren't born a hero; they became a hero. They invest time and focus and have an unwavering commitment to themselves, diving deep to explore who they are, finding strength in their gifts, and, ultimately, building a positive self-relationship.

This means that to become the superhero of your life story, you must be willing to fully embrace your journey of self-discovery, including the parts of you that sit in the shadows of your Inner Critic. This is where the largest battle often begins.

It's not easy to know what sits in the dark corners of your psyche, covered by the veil of your Inner Critic, waiting to strike when you least expect it. You can sit back and wait for the attack, always anticipating your inner supervillain's next ambush, or you can venture into those shadows armed with your superpowers of awareness, resilience, empathy, and creativity, ready for battle.

Let's start with awareness. For your Inner Champion to master its approach with your Inner Critic, it's helpful to understand how this supervillain infiltrated your inner sanctum. By tracing the footsteps of your nefarious foe, you can learn how it operates, what memories or experiences in your life it uses to keep you captive, and where it loves to hide out in your thoughts and feelings. Once you have this awareness, you have the power to form your master plan to stop your Inner Critic before it has a chance to capture you in its treacherous schemes.

What better place to start your search into the shadows than at the beginning of your life story—in childhood?

Exploring the Shadow Cast During Your Youth

The innocence of childhood: a time when we see the world through such different eyes. It's vast and filled with possibilities! All we want to do is explore, experience, and engage with everything.

And then, we start to receive feedback from that same world, telling us what we can and can't do or say, how we should and shouldn't behave, what to believe and not believe, whom to trust and not trust, and what is and isn't appropriate. That's a lot for a little mind to take in!

Along with the sheer overload of dos and don'ts is that you, as a child, didn't fully understand how to differentiate between "touching a hot stove is bad and will hurt you" and "I'm bad for touching a hot stove." All your young mind received is that you did something that upset people you love, which psychology is now finding causes young minds to think "I'm bad."

Bam! The Inner Critic finds its first opening. Though as a child you aren't likely to dwell on the thought for long, the shadow is still cast, and the pattern starts to build.

As a parent myself, I understand the importance of guiding children and keeping them away from danger. I'm in no way advocating that we give kids the freedom to do whatever they want to avoid giving their Inner Critic a window to take hold.

What I am offering is that, as you read this book, you look into your childhood and understand how these experiences may have impacted you. In doing this, you're tracing the Inner Critic back to its origin and giving your Inner Champion valuable information it needs in the battle for your focus.

As you dive into these shadows, exploring and understanding your childhood, there are two important things to keep at heart and in mind. First, you are one of a kind and so are the experiences that led you to where you are today. The possible childhood experiences we'll discuss together below are generalized, providing you with the opportunity to ask yourself, "Do I see any of my childhood in this description?" If you do, it can serve as a map to lingering shadows, but it won't paint a detailed picture.

Second, if your Inner Critic uses this review as an opportunity to weaponize memories from your past and send you into attack mode, blaming others for their wrongdoings, lean into your superpower of resilience and do all you can to resist. You may have heard the Buddhist quote, "Holding onto anger is like drinking poison and expecting the other person to die." The same is true for blame. You can spend your entire life casting blame on others and wishing they would take responsibility, but this rarely works. What it will do with certainty is feed your negative thoughts and spend your valuable time.

Now armed with your superpower of awareness, let's begin our adventure! Here are six of the top entry points used by the Inner Critic to enter your fragile childhood psyche.

- **Criticism and Judgment**: Did you grow up in an environment where criticism and judgment were prevalent, such as receiving constant criticism from parents, siblings, care-givers, or authority figures? This type of environment can breathe life into your Inner Critic as you internalize and create a harsh and judgmental inner voice.

- **Unrealistic Expectations:** Were you raised with unrealistic expectations and pressure to constantly excel or meet high standards? For example, you may have grown up in an environment where you were consistently expected to achieve flawless results. As well intended as this approach may have been by those around you, your Inner Critic could spin any perceived imperfections or mistakes into self-critical thoughts.

- **Comparison and Competition:** Was there a stage in your youth where you were regularly compared to others or pitted against siblings, classmates, or friends? This can lead to an Inner Critic that constantly has you comparing your abilities, appearance, or achievements to those of others.

- **Rejection or Neglect:** Did you ever experience rejection, neglect, or emotional abandonment during childhood, even if it was only perceived? This can contribute to feelings of inadequacy and self-blame. As a child, you internalize this as a message that says you aren't deserving of love or attention. The moment these beliefs linger, in walks the villainous Inner Critic to feed on and reinforce these beliefs.

- **Emotional or Physical Abuse:** Was any portion of your youth spent in an abusive environment, whether it was emotional, physical, or verbal abuse? This can profoundly impact the development of the Inner Critic. Abusive experiences can instill a deep sense of shame, worthlessness, and self-blame, leading to a harsh and critical inner voice.

- **Overprotection or Overcontrol:** Were you raised in an environment that was excessively overprotective or controlling? This can also contribute to the development of the Inner Critic. If you were consistently discouraged from taking risks or making mistakes as a child, it can cause your internal voice to be fearful, overly cautious, and critical of any perceived failures.

While not an exhaustive list, these entry points provide a broad sweep for exploring and understanding where the Inner Critic may have started its episodic adventure in your life and gained momentum. Take time to look and feel through each area, understanding if the shadows still exist. If any do, note it as a place to venture into once your superpowers are ready for the battle.

The Echoes of Societal Influences

Once we reach our late teens and early twenties, it's not as though we stop feeding that Inner Critic. What's more likely to happen is that we've unleashed an insatiable beast constantly asking to be fed with negative thoughts, beliefs, and self-perceptions. The more you feed it, the bigger it grows, and the more fuel it desires. It looks for validation everywhere, and societal influences give it more than enough to feed on. Being aware of these influences can help you challenge and navigate societal expectations, develop self-compassion, and cultivate a healthier self-relationship.

As you read the common societal influences below, ask yourself what role they have played or could still be playing in your day-to-day battle against your Inner Critic.

- **Media and Advertising:** Media promotes unrealistic ideals of beauty, success, and human perfection. From scripted reality television shows to filtered advertisement photos, constant exposure to these images and messages can cause you to compare yourself unfavorably. How frequently do you find yourself judging your appearance, achievements, and abilities against the unattainable reality created by the media?

- **Social Comparison:** Don't get me wrong, I love social media, but social media platforms provide opportunities for constant comparison with others. Seeing carefully curated and filtered highlight reels of others' lives can lead to a distorted perception of reality, which fuels the Inner Critic's negative self-talk. When used as a tool to lift society up, social media is a wonderful gift. But how often do you use it to compare yourself and your life with those on your feed and then tear yourself down as a result?

- **Peer Pressure:** Do you ever feel pressure from within to conform, be accepted, or meet certain social standards even when it doesn't feel like a fit for who you are as an individual? This is a sweet spot for your inner supervillain. As you shape yourself into what your social circle finds acceptable, you're now not only caught in the shadow of your Inner Critic, but also in the shadow of your social circle. Your villain has created a double lock system for its trap.

- **Educational and Religious Systems:** Educational and religious organizations that emphasize obedience, conformity, or perfectionism are a strong entry point for self-criticism in those times when you perceive yourself as deviating from the prescribed ideals. Have you ever felt as though you are somehow broken or that something must be wrong with you because you don't fit into the boxes drawn by the school or religious organization you're in? If so, this is a great place to note as you make the list of the dark and shadowy corners created by your Inner Critic.

As individuals, it can feel overwhelming to be different from the social structure that surrounds you. Blending in, even if it means fueling your Critic, can feel safer—but at what cost? When you silence your Inner Critic, embrace your authentic self, and move into a space of self-love, you're allowing yourself to find a society of like individuals who appreciate and honor you for you.

The Veil of Tradition: The Inner Critic's Cultural Armor

A shade different from societal expectations are cultural norms. They are the unwritten rules and guidelines that shape the behavior, attitudes, and beliefs of the people within a specific cultural group.

These unwritten rules include various aspects of life, such as social interactions, communication styles, dress codes, gender roles, family dynamics, work ethics, and moral values. They're learned and passed down from generation to generation and can be found in your family's upbringing, education, and broader cultural environment.

Cultural norms are embedded in more than your heritage or where you live on this beautiful planet; they live in your workplace, sports, clubs, and religious organizations. These norms provide a framework for understanding what is considered appropriate, acceptable, or desirable behavior in a particular cultural context.

Recognizing and challenging self-criticism created by your Inner Critic from these norms is imperative in cultivating self-compassion and building a better self-relationship. Here are a few examples of cultural norms to start your exploratory quest.

- **Cultural Conformity:** Have you been part of a culture that prioritizes and creates pressures to conform to cultural expectations? The fear of standing out or deviating from established norms can fuel self-judgment and a strong Inner Critic that constantly evaluates your adherence to cultural standards.
- **Hierarchical Structures:** Are you currently taking part—or have you in the past—in cultures with hierarchical structures? This may lead you to judge yourself based on

your social status or position. The internalization of societal expectations regarding your place in the hierarchy can open the floodgates for your inner supervillain.

- **Gender Roles and Expectations:** Have you been part of a culture that upholds rigid gender roles? If yes, you may have internalized messages from these cultural beliefs regarding how you or others should look, behave, or achieve based on gender. If you perceive yourself or someone else as falling short of these expectations, your Inner Critic rolls in, and the shadow is cast.
- **Face-Saving Culture:** In these cultures, there is a strong emphasis on maintaining a positive public image and taking every step necessary to avoid embarrassment or failure. Has the pressure to save face contributed to a heightened sense of fear or internal judgment for you?

There is good news when it comes to cultural norms: they aren't set in stone, and they aren't the same everywhere. They change and evolve over time. As societies and cultures adapt to new situations and influences, cultures have the power to reevaluate and transform norms that no longer make sense for everyone.

This means you can use the same superpowers you're gaining to silence your Inner Critic to become a change-maker in your culture, creating new norms. By having open discussions and questioning outdated beliefs, you have the power to shape a new culture. It's the collective effort of superheroes like you that can bring about real change and create a more inclusive and progressive world. As you do, you'll turn down the volume on your Inner Critic and the Inner Critic of future generations in no time.

Facing Down Your Inner Foes

As easy as it would be at this point to start pointing fingers and say that your Inner Critic is the sole result of external influences, deep down you know it's not that simple. Even if you grew up in an isolated bubble, having all of your needs met, that undeniable human trait of negative brain bias would still find a way to sneak in and mess with your mind, opening a chasm for your Inner Critic.

What is negative brain bias? It's a term for our brain's natural tendency to pay more attention to the negative than the positive. When we first emerged on this planet as a species, this tendency served us well, keeping us on high alert for danger in our wild surroundings. But as we've evolved and the dangers of the natural world have calmed down, our brains didn't know how to stop the negativity train, so they redirected that negative bias inward. In many ways, we've become our own biggest danger.

Let's explore how you could unknowingly be allowing your Inner Critic to wage war on your psyche using your negative brain bias.

- **Achievement-Oriented Mindset:** Do you have a strong focus on external achievements, such as career success, financial status, or social recognition? While this can be a great motivator, when you evaluate your personal value by these accomplishments, you're likely crossing into the terrain of losing self-worth and handing the reins over to your Inner Critic.

- **Need for Approval:** Are you someone who seeks constant validation and approval from others? When you rely on external opinions to define your self-worth, you can become overly self-critical when you think you're not receiving enough recognition or praise. Receiving positive feedback is wonderful and assists in building self-confidence, but when you begin to develop a dependency on that validation for your self-worth, you're bound to be battered around by your inner supervillain.

- **Over-Responsibility:** How frequently do you feel the need to take on excessive responsibilities or constantly be in control? This generally leads to self-judgment and harsh self-criticism when things don't go as planned, feeding your Inner Critic with spoonfuls of guilt, regret, and inner loathing.

- **Need for Constant Productivity:** Are you someone who believes that you must always be productive, striving toward achieving something? Do you feel guilty or inadequate when you take time for rest? In a world that rewards productivity, this is an easy cycle to find yourself in and a huge shadow cast by the Inner Critic of many. The truth is, you need time to relax to achieve optimal performance—a fact that the villain in your story doesn't want you to know.

- **Self-Imposed Limitations:** How often do you hold onto self-limiting beliefs about your abilities, potential, or worthiness? This act can lead you to self-criticism and self-sabotage when you attempt to step outside of your comfort zone.

If you saw any portion of yourself in this list, don't let it discourage you. The Inner Critic was born and nurtured by both external and internal factors, which means it can be shifted and silenced by external and internal factors too.

IN THE GRIP OF SELF-LIMITING BELIEFS

Ah, the Inner Critic—such a sneaky little voice. One of its favorite tricks is to reinforce self-limiting beliefs about your worth, abilities, and potential. It loves to whisper things like, "You're not good enough," "You'll never succeed," or "Who do you think you are?"

But the Inner Critic isn't the most reliable source of information. It's like that overly critical person in your life who always focuses on your flaws and conveniently forgets to mention your strengths. It thrives on keeping you small so it can feel dominant.

When you allow the word spells this supervillain weaves in your mind to set your limits and abilities, you might shrink away from big opportunities. You become trapped in your comfort zone, afraid to step out and explore your true potential. And just like that, you're frozen in the shadow of your Inner Critic.

Here's the truth: those self-limiting beliefs are nothing more than illusions. They're stories your Inner Critic picked up along the way and then weaved together to keep you from realizing your full potential. It's crucial that you challenge these beliefs. Start by becoming your own inner detective and questioning the evidence. Is it based on past failures or setbacks that no longer hold true? Is it influenced by other people's opinions or societal standards that don't align with your true values and aspirations?

Next, replace self-judgment with self-kindness. Treat yourself with the same understanding and support you would give to your best friend. Celebrate your accomplishments, big and small, and acknowledge your unique strengths and talents. Remind yourself that you *are* worthy and capable of growth, success, and joy.

Then, armed with this knowledge and personal empathy, take courageous steps outside of your comfort zone. Challenge yourself to experience new things, pursue your passions, and take risks. Embrace a growth mindset and do your best to see failures and setbacks as opportunities to learn and grow, not as reflections of your worth. Think about it—every person you admire right now has failed along the way. They've had to push through setbacks, pick themselves up more than once, and step back onto the battlefield with renewed vigor.

Although the Inner Critic may never completely disappear, you have the power to change the way you respond to its nagging voice. Don't let it hold you back or define your worth. You are capable of amazing things.

BATTLING THE INNER CRITIC'S EXTERNAL VOICES

Have you ever wondered why your Inner Critic's voice can sound like your high school teacher did when you made mistakes on your math test? Or your parents when you accidentally spilled grape juice all over the living room carpet?

The shapeshifting supervillain that is your Inner Critic loves to morph itself into the echoes of external judgments and criticisms you've gathered over the years. It's like a super absorbent sponge that soaks up the opinions of everyone around you: the critical, the cruel, and the downright ridiculous.

Think back to those school days when you were figuring out how to divide fractions. Maybe there was a teacher who had a habit of raising an eyebrow whenever you didn't quite get it. Your Inner Critic took that little raise of an eyebrow and turned it into a tiny voice saying, "You're not good at math."

And let's not forget those fun little parental phrases: "Don't chew with your mouth open" or "Clean your room, it's a disaster." Before you know it, your Inner Critic has morphed these little soundbites into a mental playlist that has you believing "You're such a pig!", "You're lazy!", or "You're so stupid!" Then, to have a bit more fun, this master villain puts this playlist on endless repeat, using the voices of your math teacher and parents to keep you frozen.

How does the Inner Critic get you to listen so intently to what others say and then read into it with such a negative spin? It turns out you're wired that way. Your brain loves to belong, to fit in, and to be accepted by your kind. Back in cave-dwelling days, if your cave buddies disapproved of you, it meant you would get kicked out of the group and left to fend off saber-toothed tigers on your own. Sadly, this greatly reduced your chance of survival.

Although your days of fending off tigers are far behind you, your brain didn't exactly get the memo, and your Inner Critic uses this to its advantage. Your inner supervillain has you believing there's a new kind of deadly threat—the threat to your ego. You might not physically die, but hits to your ego can be brutal. Like experiencing that awkward moment when you believe everyone's silently judging your new haircut or fearing that you might get socially canceled because of something you said on social media. Not exactly life-threatening, but certainly ego-threatening.

Add to this the research that shows your brain is like Velcro when it comes to holding onto negative experiences and Teflon when it comes to letting positive ones slide right off; you've really created the ideal conditions for your Inner Critic. That's right: we as humans tend to hold onto criticisms and judgments with an iron grip, while compliments slip away like water, leaving your Inner Critic with all the fuel it needs from every negative comment you've ever heard about yourself.

Does this mean that you're doomed to a life of negativity simply because it's how you're wired? Not at all! That's the beauty of awareness. Now that you know there's a biological link that feeds your Inner Critic's superpowers, you can use tools to biologically unlink it! You can make certain your brain gets the memo, then choose to do something different.

LEVEL 1 SUPERHERO TRAINING: AND SO IT BEGINS

At the close of each chapter, you'll dive into superhero training—a crucial phase where knowledge ignites the dormant superpowers within you. In this forge of self-discovery, you cast aside judgments of right or wrong, embracing only the valor of your personal truth.

For an immersive experience, access the free downloadable "Superhero Training Guide" at silenceyourinnercritic.com. This guide is designed to help you record your responses to the exercises and track your progress. As you move through each training, watch as your latent abilities, once overshadowed by your Inner Critic, begin to emerge.

These chapter-ending trainings are more than mere exercises; they are your awakening. Each session is a step toward revealing the superhero within you.

Confronting the Forgotten Foes of Your Youth

Reviewing the lineup of the six prime origins of your Inner Critic throughout your younger years:

1. Criticism and Judgment
2. Unrealistic Expectations
3. Comparison and Competition
4. Rejection or Neglect
5. Emotional or Physical Abuse
6. Overprotection or Overcontrol

Do you identify any as catalysts in your life? What impact(s) do you recognize they had on you? Dive deep with your response and journal it below. Your bravery in exploring the dark corners of your narrative holds the power to illuminate the trail ahead.

The Impact of Societal Forces

In your quest against your Inner Critic, how have the vast and varied forces of society shaped your armor of self-worth and honed your skills for the battle?

- Media and Advertising
- Social Comparison
- Peer Pressure
- Educational and Religious Systems

Do these societal echoes still resonate within you, influencing your stand against this internal adversary? Take your time as you either write in your journal or audio journal, reflecting deeply within.

Unraveling the Inner Critic's Cultural Crusade

In the epic saga against your Inner Critic, have the following facets of cultural design served as the villain's fuel, empowering its crusade against you?

- Cultural Conformity
- Hierarchical Structures
- Gender Roles and Expectations
- Face-Saving Culture

If so, what are three simple ways you can battle your Inner Critic's use of cultural conditions? What, if anything, can you change in your life now that you have this new awareness?

The Siege of the Self

In the vast, uncharted territories of your inner world, have you found yourself locked in an epic clash where your inner supervillain cunningly turns the following elements into weapons against you?

- Achievement-Oriented Mindset
- Need for Approval
- Over-Responsibility
- Need for Constant Productivity
- Self-Imposed Limitations

If you do recognize your shadows in this lineup, which resonates the most, and how do they shape your life today?

2. THE HERO'S TRIAL

Wouldn't it be fantastic if the voice of your Inner Critic was as harmless as a superhero sidekick's tiresome comments during an epic battle? A little annoying, perhaps, but nothing that would derail your inner superhero as you secured the safety and peace of your inner world.

Unfortunately, the saga unfolding within you is a bit more complex. Your Inner Critic isn't just some throwaway villain, easily defeated with a witty comeback or a single punch. No, this adversary is your Inner Champion's arch-nemesis who wields its power with a profound and often stealthy impact, slowly chipping away at the foundations of your mental, emotional, and even physical fortresses.

In this chapter, I'll illuminate the darkened corners where your Inner Critic plots its schemes. By bringing its subtle, yet consequential, effects into the light, you are better equipped to map out your strategy, readying yourself for the battle ahead and deciding on the maneuvers that will best safeguard your well-being.

THE STEALTHY SIEGE ON YOUR SELF-ESTEEM

Every superhero must face their arch-nemesis at some point, but imagine if that foe could shapeshift itself into a whisper, echoing through the corridors of your mind. This nemesis spotlights every insecurity you hold with its words, leaving you feeling as though you're fighting the wind itself.

You would likely recognize this antagonist if you experienced it in daily life. They are the people who ceaselessly barrage you with critiques as they wear away at the bedrock of your self-worth. When these people enter your life, you can limit the amount of time you spend with them or avoid them altogether. But when the voice wielding this power comes from within, what can you do?

Your Inner Champion must reclaim its strength, rescuing your self-esteem from the clutches of the inner villain. You can do this by learning to harness your Inner Critic's energy, transforming it from a source of weakness into one of strength, and directing it toward the life story you desire to write. By redefining the relationship with your inner dialogue, you embark on a transformative path to restore the luster of your self-esteem, allowing your worth and abilities to shine through once more.

In this epic saga, taming the Inner Critic and fortifying your self-esteem is about embracing your inner hero's journey toward a more positive self-narrative and a resilient self-image. The time has come to lift the veil of doubt, to see beyond the fog, and to recognize the superhero that you are, always have been, and always will be.

THE POWER TO SHAPE REALITY

You have witnessed how the Inner Critic, like a supervillain, thrives in the darkness, its voice a sinister echo across the landscape of your mind. Yet, what remains veiled in the shadows of this narrative is a more cunning power: the ability of these negative thoughts to transform into self-fulfilling prophecies.

Self-fulfilling prophecies are not mere spells cast in the heat of battle but stealthy enchantments the Inner Critic weaves into the fabric of your reality. With each negative prediction, this dark entity shapes the very ground upon which you build your future.

These self-fulfilling prophecies are predictions or anticipations that happen, in part or in whole, because of your belief they *will* happen. When you're bombarded with thoughts that you're bound to fail or that you're unworthy, these beliefs start to seep into both your conscious thoughts and your subconscious perceptions, influencing your actions and eventually creating the outcome that your Inner Critic had set into motion.

For example, if your Inner Critic constantly tells you that you're terrible at public speaking, you'll probably start avoiding opportunities to speak in public. Then, when a time comes that you're thrust into speaking to a group, the lack of practice, combined with the Inner Critic's constant critique, will cause you to be terrible. Is this because you're not good at public speaking? Or is it because you avoided any practice in public speaking, hiding in the shadow of fear? The Inner Critic seized the opportunity to pounce on your insecurity and used it to feed itself and your self-limiting belief, creating a self-fulfilling prophecy.

When you give your Inner Critic dominion over your thoughts and actions, it becomes a vicious cycle. You start avoiding situations that trigger fear, which then causes you to deny yourself chances to learn, grow, and prove your capabilities. This avoidance becomes your kryptonite, robbing you of precious battles where you can showcase your true strength.

When your Inner Critic's messages go unchallenged, your self-esteem takes a nosedive. You start questioning your abilities, your decisions, and your worth. This snowball effect makes it even harder to summon the confidence needed to take risks, go after new things, and embrace challenges.

It's time to explore the validity of the Inner Critic's proclamations, to confront those self-imposed barriers with the might of your inner hero. Armed with the shield of skepticism and the sword of truth, dive in and dismantle the fortress of self-doubt built by this supervillain. Embark on quests for knowledge as you methodically disprove the lies that have held you captive. With each step forward, with each skill honed and each fear faced, you'll feel your power return.

The path of a hero is fraught with trials, and you'll likely discover that you can't defeat them all. That, too, is a victory. It is in these moments of honesty and exploration that you break free from the chains of fear and limitation. You reclaim your power, not because you've won every challenge, but because you've dared to face them.

The Inner Critic may seem like an insurmountable adversary, but as you find the voice of your Inner Champion, the Critic's influence wanes. You stand at the precipice of a new realm, liberated from the constant cycle of self-doubt, ready to explore the vast potential that lies within. Here, in this expanded universe of possibility, you are the author of your destiny, free to define your path and embrace the full spectrum of your untapped potential.

THE CRUCIBLE OF CRITIQUE

In the vast metropolis of your mind, the Inner Critic looms large, a supervillain with a knack for exploiting your deepest anxieties. Armed with the dark arts of doubt and fear, it launches relentless assaults on your psyche, paralyzing you at the precipice of action. To emerge victorious in this epic conflict, you must master your inner landscape.

Your saga began at the dawn of humanity, where the fear of being kicked out of the tribe was a sentence of doom. But if you leave it unchecked, this primordial craving for acceptance quickly becomes a key source of your Inner Critic's superpowers.

Your inner battlefield often emerges in moments of raw, unguarded truth, when the opportunity to bear your soul stands before you. Your heart races, not with excitement, but with fearfulness, as the Inner Critic conjures nightmarish visions of the judgment and scorn awaiting you.

Ambitions to voice your thoughts or to unveil your genuine essence are squashed under the weight of potential ridicule. The dread of alienation, of being cast out into the social wilderness, erects walls between you and your dreams.

This creates a vast paradox: by sidestepping potential criticism, you inadvertently sidestep embracing and enhancing your superpowers. You see, every act of defiance against the Inner Critic's sinister lullabies, every step taken despite its dire predictions, is a rebellion against its chains of fear. It is in these acts that you ignite your powers. True growth doesn't bloom in the sterile soil of safety and sameness; it thrives in the bold utterance of your authentic voice as you venture into unknown lands.

The gift of our modern-day world is that rejection by one tribe doesn't mean existential peril. Instead, it can be a signpost, pointing you toward a superhero community where your unique gifts are celebrated.

The Inner Critic may darken the path with skepticism and critique, but you hold the torch to light your way. With each moment of hesitation, ask, "Is this my Inner Critic plotting to keep me rooted in place?" If it is, choose one of your superpowers to break free!

THE PRISON OF SELF-IMPOSED STANDARDS

In your grand narrative of hero versus villain, there you stand, a determined visionary, locked in the creation of what you know will be your greatest masterpiece: your superhero costume. Night after night, you channel every ounce of yourself into crafting something legendary. Each detail is meticulously sculpted, each element refined until it gleams. With a hopeful heart, you unleash your creation into the world, only to be met with silence. The chorus of acclaim you envisioned over your super suit isn't there. Disbelief and confusion cloud your mind; how could this be? Wasn't it the pinnacle of perfection?

Unfortunately, perfection is one of the shapeshifting super-powers used by your Inner Critic. What you consider perfect isn't a constant shared by everyone. For example, my perfect ice cream flavor is double dark chocolate chunk with peanut butter, but does this mean it's your perfect ice cream flavor? If you say no, vanilla is the perfect ice cream flavor, it places us in a stalemate over which ice cream is truly perfect. To me, perfect ice cream presents itself one way, but to you, it shows itself another. Who is right? In this elusive quest for perfection, your Inner Critic uses your thoughts against you.

Understand this: perfectionism is not a harmless quirk. It's a specter that robs you of peace. It drains your vitality, leaving you caught in a tempest of stress and self-reproach. The harder you chase the phantom of perfection, the deeper ensnared you become in the labyrinth of your Inner Critic. The villainous voice of your Inner Critic urges you ever onward in a Sisyphean task where satisfaction remains forever out of your grasp.

What's one small step you can take right now to break free from the Inner Critic's lair? Embrace the notion that imperfection is a superpower. Allow yourself to make mistakes and learn from them. Instead of chasing an unattainable ideal, focus on progress, growth, and learning.

Shift your perspective from fearing failure to embracing it as a natural part of the journey. By doing so, you release the grip of the Inner Critic and invite self-compassion and self-acceptance into your life. Remember, your worth isn't tied to unblemished achievement. You're worthy simply because you exist.

THE TREACHEROUS TERRAIN OF SELF-CRITIQUE

Have you ever noticed how a single negative thought can be the summoner, calling forth an entire legion of dark emotions to wreak havoc? This nefarious power is the Inner Critic's most dastardly weapon, turning every gathering of thoughts into a sinister gala of gloom.

Your Inner Critic whispers a dark incantation like, "You always mess things up. Why even try?" and suddenly every dark thought and feeling assembles. Doubt casts shadows over your confidence, shame shackles you with its chains, and guilt weighs you down like a lead cloak. Before you know it, sadness storms the scene, whipping up a storm of negative emotions that thunder through your soul.

The plot thickens as these emotions circle back to feed the cycle of negative self-talk. The emotions generated by the Inner Critic ignite more thoughts and feelings, such as sadness or shame, which add to the dark magic as the Inner Critic conjures more self-destructive whispers. It's an echo chamber of doom, amplifying each negative thought and emotion into a louder, more menacing echo.

Caught in this vortex, you find yourself in relentless turmoil, each thought and feeling amplifying the others. The incessant drone of the supervillain's doom becomes a constant backdrop to your life, a villainous theme song that disturbs your inner peace and undermines your mental fortress.

The relentless assault of the Inner Critic poses a grave threat to your mental sanctuary. This cycle of darkness can spiral into chronic stress and anxiety, with each moment of self-doubt, shame, guilt, and sadness burrowing deeper into your psyche.

As time marches on, this emotional onslaught can siege your spirit with feelings of despair and defeat, empowering the Inner Critic's narrative with each passing day. The battlefield of your mind is overrun with shadows, leaving your well-being caught in the devastating crossfire.

Understanding the Inner Critic's role in this dark cycle shifts the balance of power. It arms you with the knowledge that the voice casting spells of negativity is not your true self but the shapeshifting imposter that is your Inner Critic. With this revelation, your Inner

Champion can rise, ready to break the chains of this cycle, to dispel the darkness with the light of truth and self-compassion. Herein lies a valiant step toward claiming victory over the Inner Critic and toward turning the tide in the battle for your well-being.

CROSSROADS OF DESTINY: THE HERO'S DILEMMA

Standing at the crossroads of choice, your Inner Champion faces a moment where the path forward is shrouded in mystery. You hesitate for a moment, uncertain of what step to take next. Be it the daunting heights of a career leap, the intricate dance of relationships, or even the seemingly mundane choice of tonight's dinner, your Inner Critic seizes this moment of hesitation to cast doubt and create uncertainty in every direction. Suddenly, you're caught in its trap of inner conflict.

You find yourself fearing that each choice might be the misstep that unleashes chaos in your life. Imprisoned in the clutches of analysis paralysis, you spiral into a vortex of indecision, a place where heroes fight themselves within their own minds.

If this tale sounds all too familiar, take solace in the fact that you walk a well-trodden path. The Inner Critic thrives in self-doubt and indecision.

Confronted with choice, your mind becomes an endless battleground, where each potential outcome seems like a trap. The Inner Critic marshals its forces, driving you to dissect, deliberate, and dwell on all conceivable scenarios until your hero's spirit wearies from the assault.

When you grant your nemesis free reign over your thoughts, each unchecked advance becomes harder, causing you to lose trust in your inner knowing. Doubt undermines your confidence, your choices flicker and fade in the face of uncertainty, and discerning the path that aligns with your true essence becomes a Herculean task.

How, then, does your inner superhero escape this maze of turmoil? Start by recognizing that your Inner Critic's version of reality isn't your story. Those doubts and fears it throws your way are rarely based on facts; they're opinions and often not very helpful ones. Challenge your Inner Critic's grim narrative and forge forward with your whole heart. Replace overthinking with a focus on the present moment. When you're engaged in the here and now, there's less room for the Inner Critic to dominate your thoughts. Transform the battleground by anchoring yourself in the present, where your power flourishes.

Remember, decision-making is a superpower honed through experience. Begin with small, everyday choices, to build your strength, and gradually ascend to the greater quests that await. Embrace each decision as a step on your journey, a chance to learn, to grow, and to evolve. Should the path you choose lead astray, fear not, for the superpower of choice is yours to wield again, leading you to new experiences and options.

In the epic tale of your life, you are both the superhero and the author. With each choice made, you pen the story of your journey. It's a tale of your transcendence, mastering the art of decision with the courage to follow where your heart leads.

FRAYED ALLIANCES

When your Inner Critic has a megaphone, it's hard not to listen. And when it keeps repeating that you're not good enough, smart enough, or worthy of love, it starts to affect how you view yourself. This self-doubt can be a wrecking ball to your self-esteem, making it difficult to believe you're deserving of healthy relationships.

The Inner Critic's whispers of unworthiness can lead to building walls around your heart or withdrawing from the potential of relationships altogether. You might fear being judged or rejected, so you isolate to protect yourself from pain.

To be in a truly connected relationship, you need to be vulnerable. Vulnerability is like showing someone the pages of your diary, revealing your innermost truths. It can be scary, but it's essential for deep connections. The Inner Critic hates vulnerability. It feeds on self-doubt and magnifies the fear of being hurt. Embracing vulnerability pulls the rug right out from under your Inner Critic, causing it to do all it can to keep your emotions locked away, distancing you from opportunities to connect authentically.

The impact that this lack of vulnerability has on self-love runs even deeper. It keeps you from looking inward and lovingly seeing your opportunities for growth. You refrain from embracing opportunities as adventures in life or enjoying the process of learning and loving yourself as you gain new skills.

How do you build bridges over these relationship pitfalls? It starts with recognizing that vulnerability is a strength, not a weakness; embrace vulnerability as the cornerstone of genuine connections. Practice opening yourself up, even if it feels uncomfortable at first. Share your thoughts, fears, and dreams with people you trust. If you find that's too much too fast, be willing to share them with yourself. Write them down in a journal and look at them from an outside perspective. As you do, you'll find that the Inner Critic's grip begins to weaken.

When your Inner Critic tempts you to withdraw, resist the urge. Reach out to friends, family, or support groups. Surrounding yourself with positive influences can help drown out the Critic's voice and remind you of your value.

Finally, remember that the stories your Inner Critic tells you about relationships are generally fiction. Rewrite those narratives with your empowering beliefs. Remind yourself that you're not only capable of forming healthy and loving connections but that you're already loved. Recognizing that you've already achieved your goal, makes it easier to silence the Inner Critic and continue to build upon your successes.

LEVEL 2 SUPERHERO TRAINING: HEROISM RISING

 Elevating your journey from the foundational lessons of heroism, we now ascend to the next tier: Level 2 of your superhero training. It's time to dive even deeper into the shadows, understanding the grip held by your villainous Inner Critic so you can build your plan to break free!

Darkness Falls over Your Fortress of Confidence

In what ways has your Inner Critic, with its cunning arsenal of superpowers, initiated a ceaseless barrage of self-criticism and doubt upon the citadel of your self-esteem? Is there a montage of your perceived shortcomings that incessantly replays in the theater of your mind? If such a playlist exists, what moments from your saga have been captured and looped in this shadow reel?

Shaping Your Reality

In what ways do you allow your Inner Critic's messages to go unchallenged, creating self-fulfilling prophecies? How often do you find yourself questioning your abilities, your decisions, and your worth, and what impact does this have on your choices?

Fortress of Solitude: The Inner Critic's Barrier to Connection

How has your Inner Critic constructed walls that shield you from the strength found in vulnerability? Have there been moments when you retreated into the shadows, evading the possibilities of deep connection?

* Remember to download your free "Superhero Training Guide" at silenceyourinnercritic.com.

3. GEARING UP FOR THE QUEST

Now that we've shed light on the nature of the Inner Critic and its capacity to wield influence over your life, it's time to reclaim your power. We'll start with a set of initial steps you can readily put into action.

THE HERO'S ESSENTIALS

In every hero's journey, there's a quintessential arsenal, a core set of gadgets and gear tailored for the myriad of challenges that lie ahead. Whether it's defending your inner sanctum or slicing through negative self-talk, possessing a reliable set of instruments instills a warrior's calm and assurance in your abilities.

This collection of initial armaments is designed to fortify you in your duels against the Inner Critic. When you find yourself ensnared in its cunning traps, a swift deployment of these tools can illuminate the path to your Inner Champion. While I wield no magic wand guaranteeing instantaneous victory, these implements create an opening for a swift tactical advantage—and often, that's all that's required to mute the adversary's taunts and reclaim your dominion.

Consider this your utility belt for the soul, each tool a beacon guiding you back to strength, empowering you to stand tall amid the shadows of doubt.

Tool #1: Mirror Technique

Many of us encounter days when we stand before the mirror during our morning routines and instead of nurturing ourselves, we tear ourselves down. We become fixated on every perceived flaw, stripping away our confidence until we reach a point where we question the purpose of our efforts to get ready for the day. Not everyone reaches that extreme. Some merely wish for a certain feature to be different, or they keep their self-critique vague, saying things like, "I look horrible today."

We coexist in a world that thrives on body shame. The more we believe that we fall short in attractiveness, the more susceptible we become to purchasing products that promise to remedy our perceived defects. A multi-billion-dollar industry is propped up on the fact that we don't feel as beautiful as we are, but there's one quality that's more beautiful than anything you can buy in a bottle: self-confidence.

Please don't get me wrong, I take no issue with the beauty industry. They provide us with products that can assist in boosting self-confidence and addressing concerns that may otherwise go unaddressed. But you can't buy confidence no matter how hard you try. It takes focus, awareness, and a willingness to put in effort.

Self-confidence ranks among one of the most magnetic qualities you can possess. When someone radiates confidence and feels comfortable in their body, you can see and sense it in their presence. You're naturally drawn to them. Every perceived imperfection becomes part of their unique character, enhancing who they are and contributing to their beauty.

When you not only accept but genuinely appreciate all aspects of yourself, your self-confidence radiates. Every aspect of you is viewed with the awe it deserves—as part of your magnificent whole. Before you can arrive at this point, though, you must authentically hold self-love, and that's where the mirror technique below comes into play.

The intention behind this technique is to embrace yourself for the incredible marvel you are, completely and without reservation. Every word, thought, and action you direct toward your body carries energy. By transitioning this energy into a loving pattern, you elevate your confidence and radiate positivity!

Here's what you'll need:

- *A mirror:* any mirror will work; the choice is yours.
- *A dry-erase marker:* make sure it's dry-erase and not a permanent marker. You may love what you write, but you might not want to see it every day.
- *A tissue or cloth:* to wipe off the mirror.

Step 1: Gazing

Begin by gazing at yourself in the mirror and truly absorbing what you see: your eyes, your facial features, your body—take it all in. Dedicate at least two or three minutes to observing your features from head to toe. Initially, this could be a challenge. I've found it can take people multiple sessions before they're able to maintain eye contact with themselves and soak in their appearance without looking away. If you encounter this, it's okay. Gradually work your way into maintaining eye contact for the full two or three minutes, even if it's in five-second increments. Once you can sustain a solid two-minute connection with your reflection, proceed to the next step.

Step 2: Positive Self-Talk

As you sustain your gaze on your reflection for those two to three minutes, notice if you're passing judgment on any of your features. If you are, employ a loving affirmation to recalibrate the negative self-talk about that area. For instance, if you find yourself criticizing your hair for resembling a troll doll's frizz (this happens to be one of my critiques of myself), you can counter it with an affirmation like, "I'm truly fortunate to have thick, beautiful hair with a personality of its own." Acknowledging the good fortune in having hair as it is, while also recognizing its unique personality, allows me to find some humor and embrace the positive aspects of the feature that is also driving me crazy. If this approach doesn't fit for you, find one that does. Another approach is to say thank you for that part of your body. For example, if you have an issue with your legs, and you can't bring yourself to say something loving about the way they look, you can choose to say, "Thank you for being my legs." The simple act of appreciation can be enough of a pattern interruption to break the cycle.

Step 3: Reprogramming Self-Judgment

Once you have a positive affirmation for the feature, refocus on the area you were judging. If judgment persists, generate another positive affirmation as you progressively rewrite the script of negative self-talk. This could take several rounds of practice, depending on how long you've harbored this criticism about yourself. If you don't fully release judgment the first time, don't chastise yourself; it's entirely normal. Remember, you've likely spent years thinking about yourself in a particular way. As a result, it may take time to adopt a new perspective.

Step 4: Self-Love

As you wrap up this technique, continue to soak in your reflection, then identify three to five things that you love and appreciate about yourself. These can be physical features or character traits. Look deep into your eyes, like you would the person you love most in the world, then state these three to five things to yourself either aloud or in your mind. Be certain to make eye contact in the mirror, allowing the self-appreciation to enter your soul through your eyes. The transformation you experience when you establish deep eye contact with yourself and speak kindly is astonishing.

Step 5: Reaffirm

Lastly, as you state these three to five items that you love about yourself, what one item caused your heart to feel the fullest? Using your dry-erase marker, write this item down on the bottom of the mirror, and then the practice is complete for the day. When you start the next day, look into the mirror and read the statement of self-love that you wrote to yourself the previous day. Allow these words to resonate, then erase the statement from the day before and begin the practice again.

I recommend practicing these steps daily for at least three months. Why three months? Because it can take up to two hundred fifty-four days for you to form a new habit or behavior pattern, with the average being sixty-six days for it to become automatic. Since our goal is to build the new behavior of seeing yourself with love and appreciation, it's important to pass that average mark and get this new behavior ingrained in your patterning.

Tool #2: The Power of Thank You

Have you ever experienced a scenario like this? At work, school, or another professional setting, you've poured your heart and soul into a project, and the results are nothing short of fantastic. You receive praise and recognition from colleagues or friends as they acknowledge all your efforts and exceptional skills. But instead of soaking in the gratitude and recognition of your achievement, you brush it aside, saying, "It was luck," or "It was nothing."

This response is a classic instance of your Inner Critic working overtime, undermining your accomplishments. It's like having a backseat driver in your mind, steering you away from the path of self-appreciation. There is a simple yet powerful technique to counter this reflexive dismissal: the "Thank You" practice.

When you receive a compliment, instead of letting your Inner Critic take the wheel, take time to consciously redirect the conversation. Start by taking a deep breath, allowing this pause to provide a buffer between the compliment that may have created an uncomfortable feeling and your response. This approach gives you a moment to acknowledge your initial instinct, then steer it in a different direction.

Now, here's the pivotal move with this tool: replace that knee-jerk deflection with a sincere "Thank you." It might feel awkward initially, especially if you're not accustomed to accepting praise, but trust me, this small phrase carries significant transformative power.

When you respond with "Thank you," you're not just accepting the compliment; you're also acknowledging your effort and the validity of the praise. It's a subtle but crucial shift. Instead of brushing off your achievements, you're allowing yourself to appreciate them.

Over time, as you consistently practice this simple technique, your Inner Critic's voice will weaken. It won't have the same foothold it once did. Saying "Thank you" becomes a powerful affirmation of your capabilities. It helps to rewire your thought patterns, nudging you toward self-appreciation rather than self-doubt.

The next time you find yourself on the brink of dismissing a compliment, pause, take a breath, and choose to say, "Thank you."

Tool #3: Challenge Your Inner Critic's Narratives

You're at a social gathering. The air is filled with laughter and chatter. You're excited to join in, and then . . . your Inner Critic tightens its grip and begins to whisper, "Everyone's already talking with who they want to talk with; leave them alone," or "You're going to say something stupid and embarrass yourself." Suddenly, the excitement fades and is replaced by anxiety and self-consciousness.

What you may not know is that most people in that room are likely grappling with similar thoughts and apprehensions. The truth is social events can be a breeding ground for the Inner Critic's negative narratives. It loves to amplify insecurities and magnify self-doubt, creating a loop of anxiety that can overshadow the entire experience.

But here's where you can reclaim your power and shift the dynamic. Instead of letting your Inner Critic dictate the terms, you can become an agent of change for yourself and others. Embrace your power to influence the atmosphere of the gathering in a positive and heartfelt way. Start by acknowledging that everyone, including that seemingly self-assured person across the room, has vulnerabilities and insecurities. The smiles and laughter may be real in the moment, but each person has some type of self-doubt beneath the surface. This realization is a superpower; it connects you with the shared human experience when it comes to navigating social interactions.

Once you have your connection, take time to reframe your role at the gathering. Instead of being consumed by your Inner Critic's whispers, become an empathetic observer. Challenge yourself to step out of your comfort zone and initiate conversations. By doing so, you're not only helping yourself overcome your anxieties, but also creating a ripple effect of comfort for others who are likely feeling the same way.

What if you approach someone who seems a bit reserved and initiate a simple hello? Chances are, they will be just as relieved as you are to have a conversation starter. Your small act of courage could create a genuine connection. If this person isn't open to a conversation, you move on, knowing you extended warmth and kindness. As you extend this warmth and kindness, you'll find that your Inner Critic's voice starts to fade. Engaging in conversation shifts your focus away from self-doubt and redirects it toward meaningful interactions. The more you do this, the more your confidence grows, and the quieter that negative inner dialogue becomes.

The next time you're at a social gathering and your Inner Critic attempts to hold you back, remember that you have the power to rewrite the narrative. Recognize that you're not alone in your feelings and that your actions can positively impact both your experience and that of others. Embrace your role as a connector, and let your Inner Critic be silenced by your Inner Champion.

Tool #4: Embrace the Learning Journey

With their permission, I'm going to share a client's story with you. To respect and protect their identity, we're going to change their name and refer to them as Alex while honoring their request to retain their chosen pronouns of they/them.

Alex is a passionate artist who had always dreamed of showcasing their work in a gallery, but every time the idea nudged them, their Inner Critic would chime in: "You'll never make it. Your art isn't good enough." The fear of failure was paralyzing, preventing Alex from taking that crucial first step.

I guided Alex to a biography about a famous novelist who faced countless rejections before finally publishing a best-seller. It struck a chord—failure wasn't final; it was simply a part of the artistic journey. Inspired, Alex started viewing each setback as a stepping stone.

They realized failure didn't define them; it was feedback guiding them toward improvement.

With renewed courage, Alex submitted their artwork to a local art fair. The response wasn't what they had hoped for, but instead of retreating, they chose to learn. They sought feedback, identified areas for growth, and adjusted. Each piece of feedback became a tool for refining their craft. As Alex honed their skills, they celebrated small milestones: mastering a new technique, completing a challenging piece, or receiving positive feedback. These wins fueled their confidence. Each celebration was a testament to their progress, no matter how incremental.

Even with these new skills, the Inner Critic whispered, "If it's not perfect, it's not worth doing." Alex recognized this as a trap. They understood that perfection was an unattainable mirage. Instead, they focused on the joy of creating, embracing imperfections as part of the artistic journey. Alex adopted a growth mindset. They started seeing challenges as opportunities to learn and grow. Each setback was a chance to develop resilience. The more they stretched their abilities, the more they discovered their capacity for adaptation and improvement.

With superhero determination, Alex practiced relentlessly. They understood that each brushstroke, each attempt, was a step toward mastery. They recalled the times they struggled with certain techniques, only to conquer them through dedication.

Whenever doubts crept in, Alex responded with affirmations. "I am constantly evolving," they reminded themselves. "Every effort is a step forward." Gradually, these affirmations replaced the Inner Critic's destructive whispers. Looking back on past achievements, Alex drew strength. They recalled times when they had overcome doubts and fears. Each success story served as a reminder that they could conquer the challenges ahead.

Every night, before bed, Alex closed their eyes and envisioned their art hanging proudly in a gallery. They felt the exhilaration of accomplishment and the satisfaction of pursuing their dreams. This visualization created a positive mental image, drowning out the Inner Critic's negativity.

Alex also confided in friends who shared their creative journey. They found a supportive community that cheered them on, celebrating the highs and offering encouragement during the lows. This network became a shield against self-doubt.

I share Alex's superhero journey because it's a fantastic reflection of how an individual can overcome the fear of failure and perfectionism. It took Alex a couple of years, but they did silence the Inner Critic with perseverance and consistent inner growth. As a result, they made their way into the art gallery.

In your superhero quest, remember that every attempt, every failure, and every lesson learned contributes to your growth. Embrace the journey, trust in your resilience, and know that each step you take leads you closer to your desired destination.

Tool #5: Flip the Script

Continuing to share client stories, with her permission and changing her name, I'd like to walk you through Sarah's experience of battling her Inner Critic. Sarah's a vibrant young professional who found herself trapped in the comparison game early in her career. Whether it was her colleagues' accomplishments, friends' relationships, or even strangers' social media posts, her Inner Critic would chime in, "You're not as successful as them. You're falling behind."

One day, Sarah found herself at a company event, watching a colleague she admired deliver an engaging presentation. As she observed this colleague's confident demeanor, she couldn't help but think, "I'll never be that polished in front of a crowd."

Fortunately, she had been doing a great deal of inner dialogue work and remembered the practices she had learned, so Sarah decided to flip the script. Instead of dwelling on her self-perceived shortcomings, she stepped into her colleague's shoes and saw things from his perspective. She imagined someone in the audience looking at her with admiration, just as she looked up to him. This shift made her realize that everyone, including this colleague, has an Inner Critic whispering doubts.

Taking this moment to flip the script and put herself in the shoes of someone she admired as a role model caused Sarah to think about her younger cousin, who often looked to Sarah as a role model. Sarah then wondered, "What kind of reflection am I providing for my cousin?" This question hit home and caused Sarah to recognize that everyone serves as a role model to someone even if they aren't aware of it. Sarah wanted to inspire her cousin to embrace her uniqueness and pursue her dreams. Sarah realized that the way she could achieve this was by focusing on her own growth, becoming a reflection of what she would like to see in the world around her.

We call this superhero technique "Reflecting the Positive." When each of us realizes that our actions have a ripple effect and we can choose what that ripple effect is, we allow our actions to be a positive reflection of what we desire to put out into the world. That's exactly what Sarah chose to do from that point forward.

Instead of dwelling on her perceived inadequacies, Sarah used comparisons as inspiration. She recognized that everyone's journey is unique. Instead of aiming to be someone else, she set her focus on becoming the best version of herself. She started setting goals based on her aspirations, not others'.

When the Inner Critic whispered, "You'll never be as good as them," Sarah responded with a new dialogue. "I'm on my own path. Daily progress is what matters." This empowered self-talk silenced the negativity with a growth-oriented mindset.

Sarah celebrated her achievements, whether big or small. Instead of minimizing her victories because someone else had achieved more, she acknowledged her efforts. Each step forward was a win in her journey, regardless of how it compared to others.

She started appreciating her unique strengths and qualities. She understood that what made her different was also what made her exceptional. She focused on building a life that aligned with her values and aspirations.

Along with recognizing her strengths, Sarah offered genuine compliments to others without feeling threatened by their successes. She realized that lifting others up didn't diminish her own worth. In fact, supporting others created a positive ripple effect in her relationships.

Sarah's superhero journey reflects how comparison can be turned into a catalyst for growth. Just as you look up to others, there are people looking up to you right now, seeking inspiration and guidance. By embracing your individuality, setting your own benchmarks, and offering support to others, you can break free from the shackles of comparison and let your unique light shine.

The Hero's Essentials Summary

As we wrap up this chapter, I'd like to offer a quick list of the tools we've added to your arsenal.

1. **Embrace the Learning Journey:** Remind yourself that every successful individual, from athletes to artists, went through a series of attempts and failures before achieving greatness. Those moments of perceived failure are stepping stones toward success. Embrace the learning journey and acknowledge that each experience contributes to your growth.

2. **Challenge Your Inner Critic's Narratives:** When your Inner Critic starts to list reasons why you will fail, challenge those thoughts with evidence that disproves them. Recall times in your life when you overcame obstacles and succeeded against the odds. Create a counter-narrative that reflects your strengths and past achievements.

3. **Set Achievable Goals**: Break down your larger goal into smaller, achievable milestones. This not only makes the goal less daunting, it also allows you to celebrate successes along the way. Understand that perfection isn't necessary for progress and success.

4. **Reflect the Positive:** Realize that your actions have a ripple effect and that you can choose what that ripple effect is, allowing your actions to be a positive reflection of what you desire to put out into the world.

5. **Shift Your Perspective on Failure:** Failure is not a verdict on your abilities; it's a temporary outcome. Allow it to be a valuable feedback mechanism. Each failure reveals a piece of the puzzle you're solving. Thomas Edison once said, "I have not failed. I've just found ten thousand ways that won't work." Embrace the iterative process of learning through mistakes.

6. **Celebrate Small Wins:** Acknowledge and celebrate your small victories along the way. These moments of progress, no matter how minor, accumulate over time. They are a testament to your effort and dedication. Celebrating small wins boosts your confidence and motivation.

7. **Let Go of Perfectionism:** Perfectionism can be paralyzing. Recognize that perfection is an unattainable standard. Instead of aiming for perfection, focus on progress. Allow room for imperfection and growth. Your journey is a series of steps, and each step contributes to your development.

8. **Practice Makes Progress:** Understand that mastery comes through practice and repetition. Just as a musician practices scales or an athlete hones their skills, repeated effort in your chosen field brings improvement. Every attempt is a practice session that brings you closer to your goal.

9. **Counter Negative Self-Talk:** Challenge your Inner Critic's negative self-talk with positive affirmations. When

thoughts of failure arise, counter them with statements like, "I am capable of learning and growing," or "Every attempt brings me closer to success." Redirect your thoughts toward self-empowerment.

10. **Inspiration from Past Successes:** Reflect on your past successes, no matter how small. Remember times when you overcame challenges or achieved something you initially thought was beyond your reach. These instances remind you of your capacity to overcome obstacles and provide you with proof that you can do it.

11. **Visualize Your Success:** Visualize yourself succeeding in your chosen goal. Imagine the feeling of accomplishment, the pride, and the sense of achievement. This mental rehearsal can help shift your focus away from fear and failure, creating a positive and confident mindset.

12. **Build a Support System:** Surround yourself with supportive individuals who uplift and encourage you. Share your aspirations with them. A strong support system can provide guidance, motivation, and a reminder that you're not alone on your journey.

13. **Flip the Script:** Be willing to change things up—look at situations from a completely different perspective or do things in a different way. Put yourself in another person's place or explore a perspective in your mind that is opposite of what you would typically explore. This can both expand your awareness and give you the moments you need to silence your Inner Critic.

Think of these tools as your Superhero Starter Kit. As you embark on your journey of self-discovery, you'll gradually develop an intuitive sense of which tool to use in different situations. As Alex and Sarah realized, the awareness of what tool to utilize is cultivated through continuous use, practice, and experience.

LEVEL 3 SUPERHERO TRAINING: QUEST PROFICIENCY

 As you stand on the threshold of embarking on your heroic adventures, the moment has arrived to hone your superpowers and skills even further. Answer the questions below in your personal journal or download free journal pages from silenceyourinnercritic.com.

The Fitness Journey Fumble

You've committed to a fitness journey, inspired by goals of health and vitality. Each time you falter—a missed workout, a goal unreached—the Inner Critic pounces, framing every slip as a failure. It's the clash between your commitment to self-improvement and the Inner Critic's relentless negativity. What tools would you pull out of your Hero's Essentials Superhero Starter Kit to win this battle?

The Relationship Rift

In the quest for meaningful connections, you find yourself navigating the complex waters of a relationship that has hit a storm. The Inner Critic uses this moment to question your worthiness of love and belonging, painting the rift as a reflection of your inadequacies. It's a tug-of-war between your desire for connection and the Inner Critic's isolating whispers. Describe how you use your Hero's Essentials Superhero Starter Kit to navigate the rough waters and silence your Inner Critic.

The Power to Say No

A request comes your way, and every fiber of your being screams that it's too much, yet the fear of disappointing others looms large. The Inner Critic capitalizes on this fear, suggesting that setting boundaries will lead to rejection and isolation. It's the stand-off between your self-preservation and the Inner Critic's guilt-tripping tactics. What can you do to rise above the Inner Critic and honor yourself?

Remember to download your free "Superhero Training Guide" at silenceyourinnercritic.com.

4. EXPLORING THE DEPTHS OF SELF

Self-awareness is the compass that guides you on the path to cultivating a positive self-relationship. It's the foundation upon which all personal growth is built. When you become self-aware, you gain a deep understanding of your thoughts, feelings, behaviors, and reactions. This understanding allows you to recognize when your Inner Critic is dominating your inner world.

ILLUMINATING YOUR INNER REALM

By being attuned to your inner landscape, you're able to catch the Inner Critic in action. You notice those moments when it starts casting doubt, planting insecurities, or amplifying your fears. Self-awareness empowers you to distinguish between your authentic voice and the negative chatter the Inner Critic loves to echo in your mind.

However, inner awareness extends beyond simply identifying your Inner Critic's antics and mind games. It grants you insights into your strengths, passions, and values. With this knowledge, you can make choices that align with your true self, rather than being swayed by your Inner Critic's agenda.

Think of self-awareness as a gentle light that shines within you. It illuminates both your brilliance and your imperfections as it provides clarity. Through self-awareness, you can discern when you're slipping into patterns of self-doubt, when you're internalizing criticism, or when you're sabotaging your potential.

In the context of developing a positive self-relationship, self-awareness becomes the guardian of your thoughts and emotions. It's like a superpower that allows you to confront the Inner Critic's destructive narrative with compassion and objectivity. Armed with this awareness, you can make deliberate choices to combat the Inner Critic's negativity with self-love and self-confidence.

In essence, self-awareness is a big step on the transformative journey to silencing the Inner Critic. It gives you the strength to rewrite the script of your inner dialogue, foster a genuine connection with yourself, and embark on a path of personal growth that's anchored in authenticity and self-compassion.

Let's kick off our inner exploration with ways we can uncover patterns and triggers that keep us from self-awareness.

MAPPING THE VILLAIN'S FOOTSTEPS

Self-awareness serves as a magnifying glass, helping you clearly track the path of your Inner Critic. As you carefully observe your thoughts, emotions, and behaviors, you unveil the intricate patterns and triggers that empower this supervillain and stop it in its tracks.

Picture it as an ongoing personal investigation. By paying close attention to your internal landscape, you can pinpoint the specific situations, people, and self-perceptions that tend to trigger the onslaught of self-critical thoughts and beliefs.

For instance, our friend from the previous chapter, Alex, realized that their Inner Critic roared every time they faced a creative challenge and feared rejection. Through self-awareness, they identified that the fear of failure and the pressure to be perfect were consistent triggers. Sarah noticed that her Inner Critic frequently chimed in when she compared herself to her peers. This comparison triggered feelings of inadequacy and a sense of falling behind.

In these examples, self-awareness allowed both Alex and Sarah to not only recognize their Inner Critic's path, but to also dive deeper within and begin to redirect it. As both individuals uncovered the underlying emotions and beliefs that fueled the negative self-talk, they were better equipped to stop the Inner Critic's influence with tools and techniques they had learned.

One of the most powerful gifts self-awareness offers you is the key to decoding your Inner Critic's language. It allows you to anticipate when this supervillain is likely to emerge and why it's chiming in. Equipped with this knowledge, you can then develop strategies to cut it off before it has a chance to strike. This involves reframing your self-perceptions, practicing self-compassion, and consciously challenging the Inner Critic's voice.

Self-awareness is a powerful tool for dismantling the Inner Critic's hold. With each trigger uncovered and every self-critical thought dissected, you move closer to freeing yourself from the grip of the critical inner monologue, nurturing a more compassionate and authentic self-relationship.

CULTIVATING NONJUDGMENT

Developing a nonjudgmental and compassionate stance when observing thoughts and emotions is like becoming an impartial observer of your own mind and heart. It takes practice, but one thing I've found to be incredibly helpful is adopting a curious and open mindset. Being open to questioning and exploring everything, including your thoughts, emotions, and beliefs, allows you to delve into your inner world without the weight of harsh self-criticism. This approach is at the heart of self-awareness because it grants you the freedom to explore both your inner and outer world without becoming entangled in self-judgment. You return to your childlike state of curiosity.

Have you ever sat by a river or creek watching leaves float by on the water's surface? You observe, simply noticing the leaves as they come and go. You don't criticize the leaves for their shape, color, or size because you know they are beautiful just as they are. But you might begin to take notice and wonder where these leaves came from or how far they've traveled. You're curious about their origin and journey, not critical of them for being what they are. Similarly, developing a non-judgmental stance in self-awareness involves observing your thoughts and emotions as they flow through without the urge to criticize them, then becoming curious enough to explore where they originated.

When you notice a self-critical thought arising, rather than berating yourself for having it, you approach it with sincere interest. You could ask, "What triggered this thought?" or "What underlying belief is fueling this?" By doing this, you treat your inner experiences as valuable information rather than flaws to be condemned.

This nonjudgmental approach is crucial because it paves the way for genuine insights. Imagine if you were harshly critical of every leaf that floated by; you'd stress yourself out and miss the experience you came to enjoy. Similarly, if you're consumed by self-criticism, you're going to stress yourself out and miss the deeper insights behind your initial thoughts and emotions.

Self-awareness isn't about completely removing negative thoughts. It's about acknowledging the full spectrum of your experiences—the moments of strength and vulnerability, positivity and negativity. By cultivating a nonjudgmental and compassionate stance, you create a safe space for your full range of humanity to flow. This allows you to navigate your inner landscape with empathy, guiding you toward a healthier and more authentic self-relationship.

CHALLENGING NEGATIVE THOUGHT PATTERNS

Since the goal of self-awareness isn't to eliminate negative thoughts altogether, we shift our focus to transforming our relationship with these thoughts. Our focus becomes redesigning the structure of our thoughts to support positivity and growth.

When you cultivate self-awareness, you develop the ability to recognize negative thought patterns perpetuated by the Inner Critic. Think of it like having a warning signal that rings when the Inner Critic wages an attack. This recognition is a pivotal moment—you catch the Inner Critic in action and have the tools to trap it.

One way to trap and silence your Inner Critic is to question its validity. You don't have to accept everything that it tells you; you can take steps to evaluate the evidence and understand if the words that are spinning in your head hold any merit. Start with questions like:

1. **Is this thought based on facts?** Often, the Inner Critic's whispers are rooted in assumptions or distorted perceptions.
2. **Would I say this to a friend?** This is a powerful way to gauge whether you're being overly critical of yourself.
3. **Is there evidence that disputes this?** Challenging negative thoughts with opposing evidence can reveal the flaws in their logic.
4. **What purpose does this thought serve?** At times, the Inner Critic's negativity masks an underlying fear or protection mechanism.

By demanding proof to support these self-critical thoughts, you weaken the Critic's grip on your mindset. You're not letting these thoughts go unchallenged; you're standing up to them with a rational and compassionate perspective. The Inner Critic takes punch after punch and goes down for the count.

At this point, the magic can happen. With the Inner Critic out cold from the knock-out blows, you can actively take steps to replace self-critical thoughts with positive affirmations and constructive perspectives, beginning to rewire your mind's default responses.

For instance, if your Inner Critic tells you, "You're not capable enough to handle this project," you can question the validity of its claim by recalling a time when you did successfully complete a project. This move forces your foe to release its grip on you. Then, you hit it with a rational thought like, "If I completed that project, it would stand to reason that I'm more than capable of completing this one too." This logic knocks your Inner Critic to the mat.

Once your Inner Critic is down, you can counter its attack with supportive logic, with a statement like, "Not only have I successfully completed projects in the past, proving I can do it, but I can also learn and excel. This means I'll get better throughout this process and will be able to handle larger projects after this one is finished." Over time, this conscious reframing creates and strengthens new neural pathways in your brain, making positivity and self-empowerment easier to achieve.

In essence, your superpower of self-awareness allows you to take charge of your thoughts. Instead of being a passive recipient of the Inner Critic's attacks, your Inner Champion rises and becomes an active participant in shaping your mental landscape. This keeps your Inner Critic down on the mat for a TKO (technical knockout).

The training for this superpower requires patience and practice, but the results are transformative. Through self-awareness, you turn the tables on the Inner Critic, showing it that you're the one directing your thoughts, emotions, and self-relationship.

EMBRACING THE NEEDS OF THE INNER HERO

If you were only a creature of thought and logic, it would be simple to reprogram your thinking and move on. But you're more complicated than that, aren't you? You have emotions and human needs that can leave you feeling very vulnerable. Your emotional landscape adds layers of complexity to your hero's journey, which is fantastic and fun, but also painful and challenging. This is where self-awareness becomes even more imperative, helping you navigate this intricate web of emotions and needs.

As human beings, we're not only driven by logical thinking, we also have the driving force of our emotions. These emotions can be powerful, sometimes overwhelming, and often interwoven with our most fundamental needs. Self-awareness, in this context, helps us act as a skilled navigator, steering through the ebbs and flows of our emotional landscape.

Imagine yourself in a vast city of emotions, where each building represents a different one—happiness, anger, sadness, fear, and so on. These emotions are like signals from your inner world, communicating needs that are not always obvious at first glance.

Self-awareness is the superpower that serves as your visitor's map in this emotional cityscape. It allows you to not only identify these emotional structures, but also dig deeper to uncover their history—the information that these emotions are attempting to provide you. For example, when you're feeling lonely, self-awareness doesn't just stop at labeling it as loneliness. It prompts you to go inside and explore, "Where did this feeling of loneliness originate? What does it represent for me? Do I need connection, compassion, or time for self-care?"

This depth of self-awareness transforms you into a fluent interpreter of your emotional landscape. You begin to recognize the intricate nuances of your emotions and the messages they convey.

Being attuned to your emotional experiences isn't merely about analyzing them; it's about embracing them with compassion. When self-awareness is present, self-judgment takes a back seat and pulls your Inner Critic with it. Instead of berating yourself for feeling jealous, you observe it and wonder what it's attempting to tell you about your need for recognition or fairness. This non-judgmental stance is crucial; it provides a safe space for your emotions to unfold, which, in turn, helps you reach your underlying needs.

By deciphering the emotional code through self-awareness, you gain an empowered understanding of yourself. You're no longer on the emotional roller coaster of highs and lows; you're an active participant in the conversation they're having with your subconscious. This gives you the power to respond instead of react.

Self-awareness also serves as a bridge between insight and action. It empowers you to take steps that align with your emotional needs. If you're feeling overwhelmed and the Inner Critic's voice gets loud, self-awareness allows you to recognize that you need to set boundaries and practice self-care. If you're anxious in social situations and your Inner Critic is heightening your self-doubt, self-awareness guides you to provide self-validation with positive affirmations and challenge those negative thoughts.

With the map of self-awareness, it's easier to navigate the metropolis of emotional needs. By becoming intimately familiar with your emotional landscape, you can address your needs more effectively, breaking free from the clutches of the Inner Critic and building a stronger foundation for a healthier self-relationship.

DEVELOPING MIND-READING SUPERPOWERS

Self-awareness gives you mind-reading superpowers! Not of other people's minds, but of your own. It pulls you out of autopilot mode, a state of being where you go through life so mindlessly busy that you fall out of touch with your thoughts, emotions, and reactions.

When you've gone through life on autopilot and then take steps to become consciously self-aware, you tend to discover a version of yourself that seems unrecognizable—one molded by your Inner Critic. This is when your superpowers of self-compassion and self-acceptance come into play.

Self-compassion involves extending yourself the same care, concern, and support as you would a loved one in times of difficulty. When you're aware of your inner experiences, you can replace self-critical thoughts with self-compassionate ones. For instance, if the Inner Critic whispers, "You're not good enough," you can pause, acknowledge this is a moment of struggle, and respond with, "It's okay to feel this way. Everyone has moments of self-doubt. I'm doing my best."

It's important to remember that self-compassion isn't a free pass to ignore your mistakes or to avoid personal growth. This is where self-acceptance steps in, allowing you to embrace your imperfections while also understanding that these imperfections are part of being human. This superpower can be particularly impactful when dealing with the Inner Critic's relentless plight for perfectionism.

Self-awareness also helps you identify moments when you need self-care and self-validation. By acknowledging and understanding your emotions using self-awareness, you recognize when you're feeling overwhelmed, stressed, or simply need a break. Then you can pair this with self-compassion and self-acceptance, creating a powerful combination. When you do, it's like reaching out a hand of understanding to yourself, saying, "I see the struggle is real. Let's take a moment to rest and recharge."

In this epic journey of building a positive self-relationship, using this trio of self-awareness, self-compassion, and self-acceptance is vital. It gives you the power to read your own mind and understand your thoughts, emotions, and reactions. As you do, you move away from autopilot and into intentional and purposeful living.

THE SUPERPOWER TRIO

As a fundamental pillar of personal growth and development, self-awareness guides you into the depths of your potential. When you know who you are, not only can you recognize your strengths, but you're also more equipped to embark on a journey of growth that's authentic and aligned with your values and desires.

Then, combining self-awareness with self-compassion and self-acceptance, you begin to identify patterns of behavior, thoughts, and emotions that hold you back without condemning yourself for having them. For example, maybe you recognize a tendency to procrastinate. When you're self-aware and recognize your patterns, you can actively make incremental improvements to shift those patterns. You may choose to focus on better time management or keep a record to understand your productivity, helping you move from procrastinator to proactive achiever.

Knowing yourself deeply lets you establish activities for growth that resonate with your true desires, not just those dictated by external influences. You begin to differentiate between goals that are aligned with your values and those based on societal pressures or the expectations of others.

More than that, the use of this trio empowers you to make intentional choices that contribute to your overall well-being and fulfillment. You're better equipped to see situations, relationships, and opportunities as they relate to you, determining whether they align with your authentic self. This clarity allows you to prioritize your mental, emotional, spiritual, and physical health over your Inner Critic's voice telling you that you should do what others tell you.

As you engage in this plight to silence your Inner Critic, personal growth and self-awareness become your constant companions. They illuminate the darker corners of your psyche, helping you understand your reactions, motivations, and fears. This knowledge doesn't just lead to change; it leads to transformation.

LEVEL 4 SUPERHERO TRAINING: THE FIRST ADVENTURE

You are now ready to embark on your first superhero adventure, navigating the cityscape of your emotions. Using the prompts below, dive deep and use the superpowers you've strengthened to confront your Inner Critic.

Entering the Labyrinth of Echoes

In the sprawling metropolis of your mind lies a hidden realm, a labyrinth of thoughts and shadows where your Inner Critic has set its traps. This maze, constructed from the echoes of past criticisms and self-doubt, is where the Inner Critic thrives, its whispers bouncing off the walls, creating a cacophony that obscures your path to clarity and self-assurance.

You, the hero of this tale, stand at the entrance of the labyrinth, armed with the light of self-awareness and a map sketched from the lessons of past encounters. Your mission: to navigate the twisting passageways, decipher the echoes, and trace the footsteps of your Inner Critic to its lair, where you can confront and disarm it.

As you step into the labyrinth, the air shifts, and you are surrounded by whispers of the Inner Critic seeking to disorient and ensnare you. But you are not the same hero who once trod these paths without direction. With each step, you use the light of self-awareness to illuminate the patterns in the walls—the recurring themes of doubt, the familiar fears, and the traps of perfectionism that have held you captive in the past.

The Practice:

1. **Mapping the Echoes:** As you advance, you encounter a junction where the path forks and the echoes seem to multiply. You hear every voice that has held you back in life radiate around you. Pause here. Reflect on the voice that resonates the loudest, the one that has caused you to doubt your path more than all others. Use self-awareness to identify the source of this echo. Is it a voice from the past, a fear of failure, a self-imposed expectation, or a blend of all of these wrapped into one by the nefarious Inner Critic?

2. **Deciphering the Footsteps:** Choosing to go left or right, you follow the echoes to their source, finding signs of the Inner Critic's presence. You see clearly now how the Inner

Critic has left its mark in your life. Maybe it's in your relationships, your work, or your creative endeavors. It's etched in the walls of your memory. Although you know you can't erase this impact all at once, your superpower trio will give you the superstrength to rewrite this narrative in the weeks ahead.

3. **Confronting the Critic:** As you continue the labyrinth narrows, leading you to the heart of the maze, where the echoes converge and go silent. Here, in the silence, you find the Inner Critic. The fear you once held has faded and your Inner Critic seems less imposing in the light of your awareness. Standing eye-to-eye with your foe, reflect on the power you've given the Inner Critic throughout your life. How can you use this moment to reclaim your narrative?

4. **Emerging Victorious:** Having confronted your supervillain without fear, the labyrinth dissolves, the walls falling away to reveal the city of your mind in a new light. The journey has not eradicated the Inner Critic, but it has diminished its power, allowing your true voice to echo more clearly. As you emerge victorious, consider how this journey of self-awareness has altered your relationship within. What steps will you take to ensure that your path forward remains guided by your Inner Champion?

* *Remember to download your free "Superhero Training Guide" at silenceyourinnercritic.com.*

5. THE SUPERPOWER TRIO IN ACTION

As you navigate through the treacherous inner landscape created by your Inner Critic, reinforcing your superpower trio of self-awareness, self-compassion, and self-acceptance is key. You'll need a full arsenal of tools, techniques, and exercises at your disposal to achieve this goal. It's my job to make certain you're well-equipped for this journey. I consider myself your "gal in the chair" throughout your adventure. I don't battle on the front lines with you, but I do provide critical support through mental prowess, quick thinking, and relentless dedication. I help you rescue your inner world from the clutches of your Inner Critic with a mix of unique tools and tactical strategies. As your "gal in the chair," I'd like to continue to build your Inner Champion arsenal with tools that have paved the way to success for superheroes like you.

INQUIRY OF THE INNER HERO

Embarking on the path of self-discovery is a hero's quest. This journey inward illuminates the vast, uncharted territories of your soul. With each moment of introspection, you uncover that your beliefs, convictions, and even your core truths are not static; they are as dynamic as the life you lead. It allows you to witness your evolution, a powerful and transformative process.

Having a consistent list of thought-provoking questions can assist you as you build and maintain this power of transformation. It guides you as you delve deeper into your personal beliefs, values, desires, and motivations, assisting you as you create a better sense of self-understanding and setting a base from which to track growth and change over time.

Here's a list of self-awareness questions (SAQs) you can use to begin your exploration.

Self-Awareness Questions (SAQs)

1. What beliefs do I hold about myself that might be limiting my potential?
2. What values are most important to me at this time in my life? Why? How do they influence my decisions?
3. What brings me the most joy and fulfillment and why?
4. What fears or insecurities are holding me back from pursuing my goals? Why?
5. If I could accomplish anything without fear of failure, what would it be?
6. What negative thought patterns do I notice arising frequently in challenging situations?
7. What aspects of my life are currently misaligned with my authentic self?
8. What activities make me lose track of time because I'm so engaged?
9. How do I define success? How much of this definition is mine and how much is influenced by others?
10. What self-care practices nurture my well-being and recharge my energy?
11. What stories or narratives do I tell myself about my abilities and limitations?

12. If success was guaranteed in one area of my life, what area would I choose and why?

13. What would I like to be remembered for when I die? What legacy do I want to leave behind?

14. How do I handle setbacks, and what can I learn from those experiences?

15. What are the closest relationships in my life? How do they support my growth?

16. What would I pursue if external validation and judgment weren't a factor?

17. What recurring dreams or aspirations have I dismissed and why? Could I begin to pursue any of these dreams now?

18. What fears do I need to confront to move closer to my desired future?

19. What steps can I take to align my daily actions with my long-term goals?

20. How can I show myself more compassion and understanding in challenging times?

Explore these questions at your own pace, allowing the process of self-inquiry to gently unfold as you gain a clearer understanding of yourself and your aspirations.

HEART OF A HERO: TRAINING FOR EMOTIONAL MASTERY

In the epic saga of self-discovery, mastering the art of emotional intelligence is like unlocking a hidden superpower, and it's essential for heightened self-awareness. Here are the strategies I deploy in my private coaching practice as I train superheroes to decipher the complex language of their emotions.

These practices create space between you and your instinctual emotions, allowing you to look at what the emotion is showing you. Although this space can last a microsecond at times, this small gap steals the power back from your Inner Critic and places it firmly in your hands.

Here are my top three secret weapons in emotional mastery training:

1. **The Hero's Emotional Logbook:** Envision yourself as the vigilant guardian of your inner world, chronicling your emotions throughout your day. Identify as much as you can about your emotions in vivid detail, describing body sensations that rise like a tidal wave when the emotion is triggered, immediate reactions caused by the emotion, and thoughts that flood in and fill your mind for minutes or even hours after the emotion occurs.

    As you diligently document these encounters in your logbook, a map of your emotional landscape takes shape, revealing the patterns of your triggers and the situations that summon them. Armed with this profound self-awareness, you stand ready in moments of trial to face down your Inner Critic as it uses your emotions against you. This is your superpower: the ability to see within the shadows, to anticipate the ambush of the Inner Critic, and to step into the light of emotional mastery.

2. **The Quest of the Seven Whys:** In the heart of every hero lies a pivotal challenge wrapped in the mystery of your deepest emotions. It's where the hero finds courage from answers discovered deep within, and it can be accessed using the technique of the "Seven Whys," a powerful weapon in the warrior's arsenal.

    When the storm of a potent emotion engulfs you, pause and pose the question: "Why do I feel this way?" Capture the essence of this inquiry in your hero's book of wisdom, laying it bare before your eyes to soak in and acknowledge. As you take in the wisdom of your answer, dive deeper into the labyrinth of your psyche, asking the question once again, "Why do I feel this way?" Again, etch the answer onto the pages of your book of wisdom, allowing no shadow to hide from you.

Ask yourself seven times, "Why do I feel this way?" Each instance peels back a new layer to reveal not just the emotion on the surface, but the roots of the emotion entwined deep within your being. This sacred ritual of inquiry aligns with the ancient wisdom of the seven energy centers that spiral through your body, your seven chakras, with each chamber guarding its own secrets and stories.

Embarking on this quest of the Seven Whys helps you uncover hidden truths that lie buried deep within. This technique is a key to unlocking the profound depths of your emotional being, empowering you with the clarity needed to deploy the precise countermeasures against the shadows cast by the villainous Inner Critic.

3. **Mapping the Timeline of Your Emotional Landscape:** In nearly all hero's stories, there's a map—not of lands and seas but of the emotional odyssey that has sculpted you into the hero in your story that you desire to become. This map is your Emotional Timeline, a sacred scroll upon which you chart the emotional moments that have punctuated the narrative of your life.

To complete this introspective quest, create a timeline of your life, marking significant emotional events. This might be the loss of a loved one, the day you met or joined with a partner, or the emotions you felt in school; there's no emotion too big or small to chart on your map if it's still within you. Detail these events with as much information as you can, allowing the emotion of the moment to flow out onto the paper. This is not merely an exercise in remembrance but a ritual of release and revelation.

As you chart this map of your life's emotions, watch as patterns emerge—threads that connect certain people and places with the peaks and valleys of your emotional landscape. These recurring trends are not random; they are the ley lines of your emotional world, guiding you to understand the chain of events that have shaped and influenced you.

The goal of these exercises isn't to eliminate negative emotions or the people and places associated with them. It's to create space to observe your past emotions and understand them better. As you do, you'll begin to recognize when similar emotions are occurring, empowering you to mindfully choose how you desire to respond to them. Armed with the knowledge of where you've been, you can chart a course forward, making decisions that honor your growth, safeguard your well-being, and align with the hero you desire to become.

Emotional mastery is a superpower that equips you with super-level strength and fortitude to stand firm against the Inner Critic's villainous onslaught. It allows you to harness your inner powers to author a narrative of growth, resilience, and self-compassion, moving you toward fully embracing your inner hero.

FEEDBACK IN THE SUPERHERO'S QUEST

Embarking on a path of self-discovery requires you to gather feedback from others much like a hero in a story would seek wisdom from ancient sages, a journey both enlightening and formidable. To do this, you begin by assembling your trusted council—those individuals who are champions of your well-being and evolution. They may be family members, friends, or mentors, but what they all must be is bound by a shared commitment to see you thrive.

When you've identified your council and feel you're ready to receive their unfiltered feedback on areas where you can improve, initiate an open and honest conversation. With full sincerity, explain your desire for personal growth, your commitment to self-discovery, and your intention to gain insights from their perspective.

Asking for help can be challenging at times, so here's a tailorable framework to help you along the way.

1. **Choose the Right Moment:** Find a time when both you and the person you'd like to ask are relaxed and focused. This creates an environment conducive to meaningful conversation.

2. **Be Open and Vulnerable:** Express your genuine willingness to learn and grow. Let them know that you value their insights and honesty, but also ask that they provide feedback constructively and kindly. Consider setting a word or phrase that you both agree to use as an indicator if either of you feel as though you're not being heard or if you feel the feedback is tipping into criticism. For example, you may choose to use the word *banana,* and any time you feel the feedback you're receiving is more critical than constructive, you say, "Banana." It both lightens the mood and gets your feelings across without the need to blame or accuse.

3. **Ask Specific Questions:** Frame your questions in a way that encourages detailed responses. For example, inquire about your strengths, areas where you excel, any blind spots they feel you have, and potential areas for improvement.

4. **Listen Actively:** When they share their observations, actively listen without interrupting. Make efforts to understand their perspective without becoming defensive. Asking clarifying questions is a great way to be certain you understand their feedback.

5. **Avoid Justifying or Defending:** Feedback can be difficult to hear, especially if it points out areas where you can improve. Instead of immediately justifying or defending yourself, take time to reflect on what is said. Pause for at least fifteen seconds before responding to avoid quick emotional reactions.

6. **Express Gratitude:** Regardless of whether the feedback aligns with your self-perception, express your gratitude for their honesty and insights. Do your best to respond with a phrase like, "Thank you for your feedback," to keep the lines of communication open and flowing.

7. **Reflect and Evaluate:** Once you've received all feedback, take time to reflect on it. Consider how their perspective aligns with your self-awareness. Are there patterns you haven't noticed? Are there aspects you've been overestimating or underestimating about yourself?

8. **Decide on Action:** Based on the feedback, decide which areas you would like to work on. Create an action plan for personal growth, setting achievable goals and milestones. Remember, you don't need to act on everything, and you certainly don't need to do it all at once. Look for consistency in feedback if you have spoken to more than one individual and consider taking your first steps in this area.

9. **Stay Open to Continuous Improvement:** Feedback is not a one-time activity. Regularly seek input from your trusted sources to track your progress and identify new areas for development.

External perspectives can be invaluable in revealing aspects of yourself that you could otherwise miss. Just as a mirror reflects your physical appearance, feedback from trusted sources reflects your behaviors, strengths, and growth areas. Integrating this external input with self-awareness creates a comprehensive view of who you are and guides you toward becoming the hero you know yourself to be, one that is admired for your bravery and noble qualities.

SUPERPOWER OF MINDFUL SELF-OBSERVATION

Have you ever been around someone who is mindful and considerate of their surroundings, including the people in it? They carefully observe what's occurring and understand how their actions impact the natural flow. The entire space somehow seems better simply because they're in it. These individuals don't get upset or sidetracked if something doesn't go as planned. Instead, they flow with the rhythm of the moment, embracing whatever's happening with joy and grace.

What if you could be that person, both in the external world and in your inner world? By cultivating your superpower of mindfulness, you bring your full attention to the present moment, becoming aware of your inner experiences and external circumstances without being swept away by them.

Here are some exercises to spark your superpower of mindfulness and break free from unconscious reactivity.

- **Mindful Breathing:** Sit or lie down in a comfortable position. As you settle in, bring your attention to your breath. Without changing a thing, notice how the air feels as it fills and leaves your lungs. Connect with the rise and fall of your chest and abdomen as you take each inhale and exhale. Observe the sensation of the breath flowing into and out of your body. When your mind starts to wander, gently bring it back to your inhale and exhale. Allow yourself five to fifteen minutes to sit in this practice. By gifting yourself this time to practice the pause, you train yourself to honor the calm space within. Engaging in mindful breathing serves as a portal to the present moment. It fosters your connection to that sacred gap between thought and reaction, connecting you more deeply to the tranquility of your existence.

- **Body Scan Meditation:** The Body Scan Meditation stands as a powerful mindfulness technique, offering a pathway to deeper self-awareness and stress relief that can be done virtually anywhere. Begin this mindful journey by directing your attention to the top of your head and gently observing what you feel. As you shift your focus downward, feel into the muscles of your forehead. Encounter any tension? Allow yourself a moment of kindness to relax and smooth any furrowed areas in your brow before moving on to explore your face, jaw, and neck. Approach any stress or tension you find there with curiosity rather than judgment. Grant yourself permission to release and soften these areas, then continue the deliberate descent through your body. Your awareness, acting as a gentle guide, will lead you across the expanse of your shoulders, delving into the space between your shoulder blades, and flowing down through your arms, wrists, and hands. With each muscle, consciously let go of any accumulated tension, allowing a sense of ease to permeate. Allow this process of mindful exploration to continue down through your chest, back, and abdomen, consciously releasing layers of strain and tightness. Proceed until you've visited each muscle and region of your body, exiting through the tips of your toes. Engaging in the Body Scan Meditation fosters an acute awareness of bodily sensations, pent-up emotions, and stored areas of tension. This practice not only aids in alleviating physical stress, but also enhances your connection to your body, encouraging a state of relaxation and heightened mindfulness that reverberates through your entire being.

- **Mindful Listening:** As you engage in a conversation with someone, actively choose to practice listening fully. Put aside the urge to formulate your response and focus entirely on what is being said. Notice the tone, body language, and any emotions behind the words of the speaker. Maintain gentle eye contact and notice how each aspect of the exchange feels within you. Resist the need to think ahead or reflect on what's been said while the person is still speaking. Instead, be fully present for every word that is being spoken in the moment. This exercise of mindful listening creates a space where communication transcends the mere exchange of words. By being fully present, you invite a deeper understanding and connection between you and the person sharing the information.

Mindfulness activities serve as a sanctuary amid the chaos of thoughts and reactions, offering you a clear vantage point where you can survey the terrain of your inner world. These practices allow you to immerse yourself fully in the unfolding moment, free from the webs of external turmoil. With each session, you fortify your Inner Champion, laying the framework for decisions that resonate deeply with your core values and enhance your overall well-being. Through disciplined practice, you cultivate the strength to navigate life's battles with intention and grace.

UNVEILING YOUR INNER DYNAMICS

In the quest for self-discovery, a wealth of advanced self-assessment tools is available. These tools assist you in revealing unseen aspects of your essence and are wonderful guides to help you through the labyrinth of your inner realm. They shed light on your unique traits, strengths, values, and ways of communicating, serving as a hero's guide for your journey of personal growth.

However, as I used many of these tools on my own hero's journey, I realized that I needed a self-assessment that embraced a more flexible approach than any I could find—a medium that captured the nuanced shifts in my soul's epic tale. Since I couldn't locate what I was seeking, I crafted the tool shared below. It's designed to detail the milestones of the soul while incorporating the evaluative aspects of traditional self-assessments.

This questionnaire invites you to the threshold of your soul's complex landscape. It beckons you to take a deep exploration of your innermost realms, encouraging a sincere and wholehearted response to each question for the clearest insights.

For a comprehensive understanding of how your hero's journey has evolved, consider making this reflective practice a yearly tradition. This will not only help you track the changing topography of your inner self, but also allow you to witness the enduring impact of time and growth on your heroic expedition.

Soul's Journey Tracking Sheet

Part 1: Personality Traits

1. How would you describe your typical approach to new situations? (Use terms such as *cautious, enthusiastic, analytical, spontaneous*, etc.)
2. In group settings, do you feel more energized by interacting with others or by having time alone to recharge?
3. When making decisions, do you rely more on logic and facts or intuition and feelings?
4. How do you handle unexpected changes or disruptions to your plans? (For example, do you adapt easily, do you prefer a structured approach, etc.)
5. Are you more comfortable with routines and plans, or do you thrive in flexible, spontaneous environments?

Part 2: Strengths

1. Think of a time when you felt particularly proud of an accomplishment. What skills or qualities did you use to achieve this?
2. What activities or tasks come naturally to you (e.g., problem-solving, helping others, organization, listening, sports and athletics, etc.)?
3. Ask a friend or family member: What strengths do you see in me? Are there any qualities you admire or consider exceptional?

Part 3: Values

1. Reflect on moments in your life when you felt the most fulfilled or satisfied. What values were being honored during those times?
2. What causes, issues, or principles do you feel strongly about? Why are they important to you?
3. Imagine you're making a difficult decision. What values do you consider most before making your choice?

Part 4: Communication Style

1. When engaging in conversations, do you tend to lead with your own ideas and opinions, or do you prefer listening and understanding others first?
2. How do you handle conflicts? Are you more likely to confront them directly, seek compromise, or avoid them?
3. Are you comfortable expressing your emotions openly, or do you prefer to keep them private until you've processed them?
4. Do you find it easier to communicate through written words or through spoken conversations?

Let this questionnaire serve as a foundational benchmark, illuminating the way you transform throughout your journey. Crafted to spotlight distinct areas for annual reflection, it aims to map your growth and progression. Witnessing your evolution over time is not just enlightening; it's truly empowering.

TRANSFORMING NEGATIVE SELF-TALK

A significant aspect of self-awareness involves the capacity to identify your self-limiting beliefs and recognize patterns of negative self-talk. In this section, we'll explore how to identify and address these patterns, taking down your Inner Critic and boosting your Inner Champion.

Demystifying Mind Mirages

In the grand narrative of your inner world, cognitive distortions emerge as the crafty supervillain's deceptive lens. They warp your sense of reality, creating irrational, biased thought patterns that cast long shadows over your perception of self, others, and the world at large.

Among the shadows cast by this lens into your psyche, several distortions loom large.

- **Dualistic Dilemma (Black-and-White Thinking):** This distortion paints the world in absolutes: flawless success or utter ruin, with no middle ground for humanity's shades of gray. It's a world where not excelling means total defeat, a realm devoid of nuance.

- **Premature Prophecies (Jumping to Conclusions):** Here lies the territory of making negative assumptions without sufficient evidence. There are two types of premature prophecies: mind-reading (assuming you know what others are thinking) and fortune-telling (predicting negative outcomes). For instance, you believe that people are criticizing you when, in truth, they're discussing something else.

- **Ego's Echo (Personalization):** This involves taking everything personally, even when events or situations have nothing to do with you. For example, a friend cancels plans, and you assume it's because they don't want to spend time with you.
- **Doom's Design (Catastrophizing):** This distortion involves blowing things out of proportion and imagining worst-case scenarios. For instance, thinking that failing a test will lead to being kicked out of school and never finding a job.
- **Emotion's Edict (Emotional Reasoning):** Here, you assume that because you feel a certain way, it must be true. For example, feeling anxious about a social event and concluding that something bad will absolutely happen.
- **Tyranny of Shoulds (Should Statements):** This distortion involves having rigid expectations of yourself and others. Using phrases like "I should" or "I must" can lead to guilt, frustration, and disappointment. For instance, believing you should always be perfect and never make mistakes.

If you recognize yourself in any of these mind mirages, fear not! This is the first stride toward disarming the shadows created by your Inner Critic. When you find yourself caught in distorted thinking, the next step is to pull out your munitions and stand strong in the face of this villainous foe. Here are a few more armaments to add to your arsenal.

- **Seek the Truth (Reality Check):** Question the foundation of your thoughts—are they built on fact or fiction? Is there concrete evidence for what you're thinking? If there is, what can you do to make lasting changes? If not, then recognize the pattern and use one or several of the self-awareness tools in the previous section to reconnect with yourself and the present moment.

- **Explore Alternatives (Alternative Explanations):** Consider other explanations for the situation. Are there other reasons why something happened or is happening, besides the negative one you're assuming?
- **Friend's Counsel (Perspective Shift):** Consider the advice you'd give a friend facing a similar situation. Often, the counsel you would give to others shines a light on the path you yourself should take.
- **Shades of Reality (Balanced Thinking):** Find the gray area between extremes. Instead of thinking in black and white, acknowledge the nuances in a situation. Rarely in life are things black and white.
- **Champion's Chant (Positive Affirmations):** Counter the Inner Critic's venom with truths that affirm your worth, strength, and capacity for growth.
- **Proof against the Night (Evidence Gathering):** Collect evidence that challenges your distorted thoughts. Look for instances where your negative assumptions were proven wrong.

By identifying and challenging your cognitive distortions, you shift the lens of falsification set by your Inner Critic. You direct light into the darkness, seeing things once concealed by this super-villain's negative narrative. As you do, self-limiting beliefs begin to lift, and the way you view life takes on a new perspective.

The Super Skill of Transformation

It's a striking reality that while negative comments from others can be unwelcome, we often subject ourselves to far harsher inner criticism without making efforts to alter this pattern. The time for change is now.

Embrace this opportunity to awaken your Inner Champion and alter your self-defeating dynamic. Spark the superpower that transforms negative self-talk into a more nurturing and positive inner dialogue.

Among the potent abilities at your disposal, the power of conscious choice shines brightly. By replacing self-deprecating thoughts with expressions of self-compassion and support, you harness the power to not only modify the way you speak to yourself, but also how you view yourself.

Below, you'll find a collection of positive affirmations designed to initiate this transformative journey. View these affirmations as your foundational runes, a set to be tailored and built upon to suit your needs.

POSITIVE AFFIRMATIONS LIST

1. I learn and grow from challenges.
2. I am worthy of love and acceptance just as I am.
3. I am resilient and can handle whatever comes my way.
4. I treat myself with kindness and respect.
5. I am constantly improving and evolving as a person.
6. I trust in my intuition and make choices that align with my values.
7. I am in direction of my thoughts, and I choose positivity.
8. I let go of comparisons and focus on my unique journey.
9. I am deserving of success and achieving my goals.
10. I am enough, just as I am, without needing to be perfect.

Choose the affirmations that resonate with you the most and adapt them to your situation. Using positive reframing statements consistently will gradually transform your inner dialogue and foster a more supportive and compassionate self-relationship.

EQUIPPING YOUR INNER CHAMPION

As we conclude this vital chapter, we've traversed the realms of self-awareness, self-compassion, and self-acceptance, gathering an arsenal of tools designed to fortify your Inner Champion against the assaults of the Inner Critic. From this vantage point as your "gal in the chair," it has been my privilege to guide you through this labyrinth, ensuring that every weapon, shield, and piece of armor in your armory is not only understood but mastered. These tools are more than simple strategies; they are the keys to unlocking the full potential of your inner hero, allowing you to navigate the challenges of life with resilience and grace.

In our journey, we dove into practices that illuminate the inner workings of your mind, heart, and spirit, fostering a profound connection to the core of your being. We've explored techniques that transform self-criticism into self-encouragement and learned to view ourselves through lenses of kindness and acceptance. Each practice and exercise has been a stepping stone toward reinforcing your inner sanctuary—a place where your Inner Champion stands strong.

As you continue down your path, remember that these tools are in your arsenal for your lifetime of adventures. Your inner landscapes will change, and new challenges will arise, but with your armory built, you're prepared. Your "gal in the chair" will be cheering you on every step of the way, confident in the knowledge that within you lies a superhero, ready to embrace each moment with courage, compassion, and unwavering self-acceptance.

LEVEL 5 SUPERHERO TRAINING: USING YOUR ARSENAL

You've added several new resources to your armory; now it's time to use them in different scenarios. How would you use your superpowers, along with your arsenal of tools and techniques, to silence the Inner Critic?

Dismantling the Myth: "Success Is Beyond My Reach"

The Critic's Challenge: Deep down, you harbor the belief that true success—whether in your career, personal projects, or relationships—is unattainable for someone like you. This prison of belief, put in place by your Inner Critic, keeps you from going after what you desire because you're afraid of failing. Even worse, this supervillain has also cast fear on the possibility of achieving success. You're frozen.

The Mission: What can you do to break free from this myth?

Changing the "I Can't Change" Paradox

The Critic's Challenge: After years of failed attempts to adopt healthier habits, you've resigned yourself to the belief that you can't change. Your Inner Critic has convinced you that you're someone who doesn't have the discipline for a healthier lifestyle, so why bother?

The Mission: What are specific ways your Inner Champion can take down the false narrative created by your Inner Critic?

Unlearning the "I Can't Learn New Things" Lie

The Critic's Challenge: You've convinced yourself that you're not able to pick up a new language, believing that being multi-lingual is reserved for those who are much more worldly and intellectual than you. This mindset has kept you from pursuing interests, growth opportunities, and even travel.

The Mission: List three tools from your superhero arsenal that you can use to combat this lie and move forward with achieving your goal.

Remember to download your free "Superhero Training Guide" at silenceyourinnercritic.com.

6. YOUR BATTLE ARMOR

Do you recall the strategy of Flipping the Script? This technique involves examining situations from entirely new perspectives and integrating these insights into your life as you adapt and grow. Unfortunately, your Inner Critic has mastered this super skill too, using it to undermine your progress along your superhero journey. As you start down your path of liberation from its nefarious influence, the Inner Critic adapts, scrutinizing your triumphs and leveraging them to sow seeds of doubt. This villain's ability to adapt is why nurturing self-compassion is a key component of your battle armor.

Here you stand, ready to face off against your inner villain. You've spent five chapters understanding the origin story of this cunning critic, the powers it possesses to shapeshift and use your own mind against you, and you've plotted a map of where it hides in the shadows of your psyche. You've also uncovered your hidden superpowers, gathered an arsenal of tools to combat its attacks, and learned how to reinforce your knowing of self. Now, as you prepare to step even further inward and go head-to-head with this dastardly foe once again, it's time to reinforce your super suit with true magic—the magical enchantment of self-compassion. This enchantment superpower encompasses:

- A sympathetic awareness and concern for your suffering;
- A willingness to witness and be emotionally moved by that suffering, not suppress or ignore it;
- And then a desire to take action to remove your suffering.

Venturing into the realm of self-compassion may feel like navigating uncharted waters, especially when stepping out from under the long shadow cast by the Inner Critic. But embracing this potent magic is important in safeguarding your spirit, healing from past wounds, and reclaiming your power. As you embark on this journey, embrace three foundational steps to summon the protective magic of self-compassion, fully embrace this superpower, and turn the tide in this epic battle.

THE THREE-STEP TRANSFORMATION

In the quest for reclaiming your inner realm, simplicity becomes the guiding light. As the strategist behind the scenes, your "gal in the chair," my mission is to arm you with tools that not only enhance your journey, but also simplify it. Here are three simple steps you can take to reinforce your armor of self-compassion.

1. **Love Yourself as You Are While Moving toward Who You're Becoming:** The essence of self-compassion lies in wholeheartedly loving and accepting yourself every step of the way. This love and acceptance forge a deep connection to your true self, celebrating your individuality, free from external expectations. It's a recognition of your inherent worth as you navigate the evolving landscapes of your inner world and your consistent progress. This step is about acknowledging your present self while also being open to the endless possibilities that each new day brings.

2. **Honor Your Boundaries with Reverence:** Treating yourself with respect is like setting up a security system that

guards your well-being. It involves drawing clear boundaries, dedicating time to self-care, and placing a premium on your desires and dreams. Each thought and action toward yourself sends a signal to the universe about how you desire to be treated by others. Ensure these signals mirror the respect and consideration you seek.

3. **Celebrate Your Essence with Gratitude:** Make it a ritual to honor your achievements, acknowledge your strengths, and reflect on the hurdles you've surmounted. This practice not only bolsters your self-esteem, but also magnifies your capacity to appreciate and accept accolades from the world. It's about recognizing the valor and resilience within, celebrating the victories, both monumental and minute, that mark your journey.

These pillars of self-compassion lay the groundwork for an invincible inner sanctum where emotional resilience flourishes.

VANQUISHING THE VILLAIN'S SIDEKICKS

You begin the ritual to call forth your self-compassion when, suddenly, you're confronted by not only the echoes of your Inner Critic, but also its villainous sidekicks: doubt, fear, guilt, and shame. These dastardly comrades set mazes and traps in your mind, using your thoughts against you like a house of mirrors. But there is a way to defeat these sidekicks. With consistent use, the techniques below are designed to vanquish them, opening the gateway for you to summon your self-compassion.

Speak to Yourself with Love and Kindness

In the quest to vanquish the shadows cast by your Inner Critic's notorious sidekicks, it's crucial to master the language of love and kindness within the realm of your mind. Aspire to speak to yourself with the same tenderness and respect that you wish to receive from the world. The journey to self-compassion begins with mindful practice of your inner dialogue. Below are strategies to guide you in nurturing this self-speak.

Self-Listening Exercises

Set aside a specific time in your day to create a quiet space and simply listen to your thoughts without judgment or a need to put them into motion. It can be five minutes or thirty minutes; whatever you feel you can do. Unlike meditation, where the goal is to quiet the mind or focus on a single thought, this practice is intended to let your thoughts run free, listening to all of them as they arise without jumping ahead or getting to the next thing.

As you give yourself this time to observe your thoughts, you might find that the constant mind chatter during other parts of your day slows down. When your mind feels like it will have your undivided attention at some point throughout the day, it's willing to wait for that dedicated time to share its thoughts.

Self-Gratitude Phrases

Take a few moments now to build out five to seven self-gratitude phrases. Self-gratitude phrases are easy-to-remember sentences that you tell yourself when you've done something well. For example, a self-gratitude phrase could be, "I'm grateful for my ability to stay calm in chaotic situations." Then, when you find yourself in a chaotic situation, you say this phrase to reinforce this piece of your self-compassion armor. With this act, you keep your Inner Critic from using chaos to pop in and create a running dialogue.

Meditate and Explore Your Inner Landscape

As you continue to build your positive self-relationship, exploring the terrain of your inner world is important. To know your authentic self, you need time to sit quietly and traverse inward. After all, how do you truly get to know a new person in your life? Generally, you spend time with them, both alone and in group settings, at various times of the day and night. You ask them questions about themselves, observe their behaviors and actions, and invest time in the relationship. Why would it be different when building a relationship with yourself?

Meditation is a great tool to create distance between you and your thoughts, allowing you to ask yourself questions and observe your behaviors. It helps you look at yourself from the outside without harsh judgment.

Here are a few meditations to consider. I'll write each meditation out in detail so you can practice them with friends and family, but the audio versions are also available online at silenceyourinnercritic.com.

Self-Reflection and Expansion Meditation

In this self-reflection and expansion meditation, you'll have an opportunity to reflect on mistakes in your life and view them differently. You can transform the way you see these moments and embrace them as growth rather than dwelling on self-criticism. To do this, find a quiet and comfortable space where you won't be disturbed. Sit or lie down in a relaxed position, close your eyes, and take a few deep breaths to settle your mind. Once you're relaxed, gradually allow yourself to follow these steps:

Step 1: Awareness of Mistakes

Begin by gently recalling a recent mistake or perceived failure. Allow yourself to fully acknowledge the situation and any emotions that arise. Notice any self-critical thoughts that surface.

Step 2: Detached Observation

Now, imagine stepping back from the situation and observing it as though it were a scene in a movie playing in a large theater. View it from an outsider's perspective, without judgment or self-blame. Watch it play out on the big screen like you're a character in a scene that happened separate from you.

Step 3: Recognizing Lessons

As you observe the situation, start to see the situation in a new way; identify any lessons or insights you can draw from it. What did you learn from this experience? How can this situation contribute to your personal growth and development? Shift your focus from self-criticism to curiosity about how this event can contribute to your character development.

Step 4: Reframing Mistakes

Visualize mistakes as a plot development that contributes to the larger motion picture of your life. Even though it may not make perfect sense right now, it's an essential part of the storyline that is the entire film. You may not know exactly where it's going to lead you, but you know that it's pivotal to the storyline.

Step 5: Growth and Acceptance

Repeat this to yourself: "I embrace every step in my life as an opportunity for growth. I release self-criticism and choose self-compassion. I am evolving and learning with each step I take."

Step 6: Expanding Perspective

Gradually expand your focus to other areas of your life where you feel you've made mistakes. Apply the same process of detached observation, recognizing lessons, and reframing the scene. See how these experiences have shaped who you are today.

Step 7: Future Intentions

As you conclude the meditation, set an intention to approach missed steps with an open heart and a growth mindset. Remind yourself that every step, including missed steps, contributes to your journey.

Step 8: Gratitude and Closure

Take a few deep breaths and express gratitude for the insights gained from this meditation. Slowly open your eyes and carry this expanded perspective with you as you go about your day.

Mistakes are a natural part of being human. They offer valuable opportunities for learning and growth. Through this meditation, you can shift your perspective and culti-vate self-compassion, allowing yourself to embrace your journey with open arms and an open heart.

The Voyage Within: A Meditation for Self-Discovery

In the epic tale of self-transformation, the practice of self-discovery meditation emerges as a powerful artifact, capable of illuminating the hidden depths of your inner universe. This sacred ritual invites you to embark on a journey of profound self-awareness and to forge a bond of unity with your core essence.

Step 1: Grounding

Find a quiet and comfortable place where you won't be disturbed. Close your eyes and take a few deep, calming breaths. Let go of any tension in your body with each exhale. As you relax, imagine yourself standing in a peaceful place in nature. Feel the solid ground beneath your feet. Visualize roots extending from the soles of your feet, growing deep into the earth, grounding you to your core.

Step 2: Letting Go

Imagine that wherever you are in nature, there's a gentle stream flowing nearby. As you watch the stream, you collect all of your worries, expectations, and external pressures together and place them into the water. You watch as they float away, leaving you feeling lighter and free.

Step 3: Enter Your Inner Sanctuary

With the weight of your worries, expectations, and external pressures floating away, you now see a door appear. It's as if it's hovering in the middle of nature, waiting for you to open it. You approach the door and open it to find a warm, welcoming space within. This is the gateway to your inner sanctuary—your sanctum. You step inside and take a moment to feel its comfort.

Step 4: Reflecting on Your Journey

As you look around, you find a comfortable sitting area, sit down, and recall moments from your past. These are moments when you felt truly alive, joyful, and at peace. These could be simple memories or significant experiences. You allow yourself time and space to fully relive these moments, feeling the emotions they evoke.

Step 5: Exploring Your Values

As these memories and experiences subside, you ask yourself, "What truly matters to me? What do I value most in life? When my time in this world is complete, what will I have been grateful to have experienced?" Let your mind freely explore these questions. Don't rush. Listen to your heart's response.

Step 6: Uncovering Passions

As you continue forward in the meditation, ask yourself, "What activities make me lose track of time, giving me a sense of flow and fulfillment? How do these activities ignite my passion and spark purpose within me? Is there an opportunity to include them in my life more frequently?"

Step 7: Embracing Your Strengths

Now begin to think about your strengths—your unique talents, qualities, and skills. What achievements are you proud of and how did your strengths contribute to them? Acknowledge that these strengths are a part of who you are.

Step 8: Embracing Imperfections

Reflect on your perceived flaws or any aspects you've been critical of. What are ways you can recognize these traits are part of what makes you a diamond and beautifully unique?

Step 9: Loving and Accepting Your Present Self

As you continue to reflect on your perceived flaws, you feel guided to stand in front of a mirror in your sanctuary. You gently stand up from your seat and move over to a full-length mirror leaning in the corner. Here, you gaze into your eyes and say, "I love and accept myself completely and unconditionally. By loving and accepting myself completely and unconditionally, I open the gateway for others to do the same."

Step 10: Setting Intentions

Before you leave your inner sanctum, take a moment to set an intention for your journey of self-awareness. It could be something such as, "I will continue to explore and embrace who I am with gentleness, love, and kindness."

Step 11: Returning

Slowly become aware of your physical surroundings by making small movements of your fingers and toes. Move your head from side to side. And when you're ready, take a few deep breaths, then open your eyes.

This journey of self-discovery is paramount for your inner superhero. It ensures that you stand firm in your power, grounded in the knowledge of your current strengths, while also keeping your eyes on the distant peaks of growth and evolution. Engaging with practices like this meditation allows you to know yourself deeply and unlock the true scope of your capabilities. You can stand ready to face the world with a heart full of courage and a spirit poised for adventure!

The Path to Redemption: A Meditation of Self-Forgiveness

In the heroic journey of life, it's common for dedicated superheroes to become their own harshest critics. You entangle yourself in webs of guilt and remorse, replaying your missteps and perceived failings over and over in your mind with a severity you would never direct at another. It's in these moments that the power of self-forgiveness becomes your most crucial ally in building the self-compassion piece of your armor, keeping the Inner Critic and its band of mischievous sidekicks from taking over your thoughts.

Below is a guided meditation of self-forgiveness, a sanctified rite designed to guide you back to inner peace and foster a deep, healing connection with your heart. This sacred practice serves as a beacon, illuminating the path to forgiving yourself and nurturing the garden of self-compassion within.

Step 1: Setting an Intention

Begin by finding a comfortable and quiet space. Sit or lie down in a relaxed position. Close your eyes and take a few deep breaths, inhaling through your nose and exhaling through your mouth. Once you are comfortable and relaxed, take a moment to set your intention for this meditation. You could say to yourself, "During this meditation, I will allow myself personal forgiveness, and I will let go of any self-blame." The key to setting your intention is to make certain it is personal to you and connects deeply with you.

Step 2: Cultivating Breath Awareness

Bring your attention back to your breath. Notice the gentle rise and fall of your chest and abdomen as you breathe in and out. Let your breath become a soothing rhythm that anchors you to the present moment.

Step 3: Self-Reflection

Bring to mind a specific mistake or decision that you've been holding onto. Without judgment, allow the memory to arise. Acknowledge any emotions that come along with it.

Step 4: Offering Understanding

Now begin to invoke your imagination. Visualize yourself sitting across from a replica of you. This replica is a kind, gentle, and loving version of you, who is there to listen. You speak with your replica, sharing the specific details of the mistake or decision that you've been holding onto as the replica listens empathetically. You pour your heart out to your replica, sharing everything you've ever thought or felt about this mistake or decision. As you do, you notice your replica looks back at you with nothing but love and compassion for the pain you've been feeling.

Step 5: The Power of Imperfection

Once you've shared all that you have to share with your replica, your replica looks at you with pure love and gently reminds you that imperfection is a shared human experience. Your replica comes close to you, embracing you in a hug as it whispers in your ear, "You're not defined by your mistakes. You're growing and learning. Imperfection is part of the journey." As you hear these words echo in your mind, your replica fades back into you.

Step 6: Cultivating Self-Compassion

To anchor this acceptance into yourself, you place your hand over your heart. With each breath, you inhale self-acceptance and exhale self-criticism. Repeat this phrase silently or aloud: "I forgive myself. I offer myself love and understanding."

Step 7: Visualization of Release

Once you feel the roots of self-compassion taking hold, envision there's a deflated balloon in your hands. As you inhale, imagine you're pulling any guilt, shame, or self-blame that continues to linger in your body into your lungs and then, as you exhale, blowing it out into the balloon. Continue this process, inhaling and gathering all guilt, shame, and self-blame into your lungs, then exhaling it into the balloon. With each exhale, you notice the balloon somehow becomes lighter.

Step 8: Letting Go

Once you've exhaled your last bit of guilt, shame, and self-blame into your balloon, visualize releasing it into the sky. Watch it float away, carrying with it the guilt, shame, and self-blame you had held inside. As it disappears, say to yourself, "I release all of the guilt, shame, and self-blame I have been carrying for so long. I forgive myself fully and love myself completely."

Step 9: Reinforcing Self-Forgiveness

Silently repeat these affirmations:

- I forgive myself fully and completely.
- I love all aspects of who I am.
- I am free from the chains of guilt, shame, and self-blame.

Step 10: Returning to the Present

Gently bring your awareness back to your breath. Feel the rise and fall of your chest and abdomen. Make small movements of your fingers, toes, and head. When you're ready, open your eyes.

Each time you engage in this meditation, you're nurturing a deeper sense of self-compassion and allowing yourself to heal from within.

Recent studies in the field of mental health are finding that self-compassion is one of the best entry points for building self-esteem. When you provide yourself personal grace and support in times of suffering, you create a pathway where you recognize your accomplishments. As a result, you feel more certain of your ability to overcome obstacles and handle any situation. Your armor of self-compassion suddenly not only invokes your superpower of self-esteem, it also sparks your powers of self-knowing and self-trust.

LEVEL 6 SUPERHERO TRAINING: ARMOR ON

Before we send you into the metropolis of your memories and shadowy alleyways of your insecurities, where your Inner Critic and its sinister sidekicks hide out, we're going to reinforce the section of your armor that is self-compassion with these training drills.

Navigating Personal Conflict

Situation: A misunderstanding with a close friend leaves you feeling guilty and questioning your actions. Using methods you learned in this chapter, what can you do to look at the situation from all sides, creating self-compassion while also understanding where you may have a growth opportunity?

Overcoming a Setback

Situation: An ambitious personal goal falls through, leaving you doubting your capabilities and worth. Choose at least two methods you learned in this chapter to reinforce your armor of self-compassion and move through the setback.

The Work Presentation Challenge

Situation: You're tasked with leading an important presentation at work, and the fear of judgment and failure looms large. What can you do to armor up and walk into that presentation with full confidence, persevering over the Inner Critic?

* Remember to download your free "Superhero Training Guide" at silenceyourinnercritic.com.

7. THE SHOWDOWN BEGINS

It's time to unleash your authentic hero within. Everything you've read and practiced up to this point has been training you for the showdown you're about to face. In the next several chapters, battle lines will be drawn between your Inner Champion, your Inner Critic, and those who feed it.

You will go one-on-one in the metropolis of your mind, using the superpowers you've honed and the armor you've reinforced. The dark alleys, held captive by doubt and fear, will be replaced with clearly lit pathways of personal boundaries and guiding principles. The venom of negative self-talk will be replaced with the sweet song of love for self and others. It's time to set out on your hero's journey and emerge victorious.

UNLEASH YOUR AUTHENTIC HERO

As your Inner Champion rises, you'll find you can embrace and embody your authentic self, even in the face of external pressures that push you to conform. You'll have the strength to be honest and transparent, both with yourself and with others, while also accepting accountability for any missed steps along the way.

Through this authenticity, your values, beliefs, and behaviors come into alignment, creating a coherent and integrated sense of self. In essence, you'll have created an impenetrable inner fortress against your Inner Critic.

You've awakened your inner hero by championing and expressing your deepest knowing of who you are, freeing yourself from societal expectations or pressures. Authenticity has led you to greater self-acceptance, sparking you into becoming your own Inner Champion.

How do you continue to embody your inner superhero as you enter this showdown with your Inner Critic? What do you do when this supervillain seemingly spins the world against you? Here are a few tips to help you power up as you prepare to face-off.

Developing Resilience in the Face of Judgment

Let's revisit the hero's journey of Alex, the passionate artist we discussed earlier in these pages. Alex has a heart full of creativity and a soul that thrives on self-expression. This valiant superhero had always felt a deep connection with art, channeling their deepest emotions into masterpieces that reflected their life. But, like many artists, Alex often battled with a crippling fear of being judged for their work.

One day, Alex decided to go toe-to-toe with this fear and showcase their art at a local gallery. Using the superpowers they had uncovered in their training, Alex moved through the fears that arose with mindfulness, meditation, and self-compassion, until the day of the show finally arrived. As Alex set up their pieces, excitement mingled with nervousness. The gallery's visitors were known for their discerning taste and candid critiques. The overwhelming fear of judgment crept in: What if their art wasn't good enough? What if people criticized their style or questioned their abilities? Were they truly strong enough to withstand this battle?

The opening night was underway, and as guests flowed into the gallery, Alex's heart raced. They watched as people paused in front of their artwork with unreadable expressions. Soon, whispers filled the air, and Alex couldn't help but imagine the worst.

Among the crowd was an elderly gentleman. He studied each piece with an intensity that caught Alex's attention. Eventually, the man approached Alex, his eyes twinkling with an unexpected warmth.

"Alex, your art," he began, "it tells stories that resonate to the very core of my soul. It's as if each piece you created whispers from your heart and speaks directly to mine."

Alex was taken aback by his genuine appreciation. The gentleman went on to explain that he, too, had been an artist once, but he had let the fear of judgment stifle his passion. As he spoke, Alex saw themselves in the story he shared. Suddenly Alex realized they were allowing fear of judgment to stifle their experience of the exhibit they had worked so hard to achieve. Alex decided to invoke their superpower of self-awareness and reengage in the showcase in a new way.

As the exhibition continued, Alex encountered a mix of reactions. Some praised their work, while others offered critical feedback. In the past, negative comments would have shattered Alex's confidence, but this time was different. They had a newfound resilience.

With each critique, Alex found themself asking, "Is this feedback constructive? Does it help me grow as an artist?" Alex reminded themselves to distinguish between genuine suggestions for improvement and baseless negativity.

The exhibition's end marked a turning point for Alex. They realized the fear of judgment couldn't define their artistic journey. Instead of succumbing to self-doubt, they embraced resilience. Alex continued to create, pouring their heart into their art without the weight of external judgment holding them back.

It can be easier to know how to walk the hero's path when you've witnessed another's journey. I've used Alex's story as a practical example of how these tools can be applied in a real-life situation. In Alex's journey, the following tools and superpowers played a pivotal role.

- **Pause and Reframe:** When confronted with critique, Alex demonstrated the power of taking a moment to pause and reframe the situation. Instead of immediately internalizing the feedback, Alex stepped back to evaluate its value. They asked themselves whether the comments were constructive and could contribute to their growth. This practice allowed Alex to filter out baseless negativity and focus on feedback that had the potential to aid their progress. By discerning between unhelpful criticism and genuine suggestions, Alex used the feedback as a tool for learning and improvement.

- **Seeing Self in Others:** Alex's willingness to recognize a reflection of themselves in the gentleman is a testament to their self-awareness. This ability to see a part of their own identity mirrored in someone else provided Alex with an external perspective on their tendencies. Through this lens, Alex gained insights into their own behavior and reactions. In the context of judgment, this perspective shift empowered Alex to understand that the opinions of others wouldn't define their journey as an artist. It reinforced the idea that their worth and talent transcended external opinions.

By pausing to assess and reframing their perceptions, Alex harnessed their strength to filter out negativity. Embracing the practice of recognizing oneself in others enriched Alex's self-awareness and empowered them to navigate judgment with resilience and self-assurance. This example serves as a reminder that these tools are not mere theories but practical instruments for fostering personal growth and a positive self-relationship.

MOVING BEYOND THE VILLAIN'S STORYLINE

In the storyline crafted by your Inner Critic, external praise and validation are needed to cultivate a sense of self-worth. Without constant streams of external reinforcement, our inner realm falls apart. This external dependency allows the inner supervillain to direct and dominate our internal feelings of worth and self-acceptance.

For most of us, the tricky part isn't in recognizing the need to reduce our dependence on external validation, it's in understanding how to start breaking the dependency that eludes us. Think back to a time when you received praise or recognition for an accomplishment. It felt warm and exhilarating, didn't it? Much like a hero's welcome after a victorious battle. Unfortunately, this euphoria is fleeting, leaving a craving for the next triumph, the next round of applause. It can quickly create a ceaseless quest for external recognition, a vicious cycle where the Inner Critic thrives.

If you're seeking praise that doesn't come, for any number of reasons, then the Inner Critic whispers to you, "See, you've failed. Nobody noticed and nobody cared." This sense of failure builds the longer you go without praise or validation. Before you know it, your Inner Critic has you trapped in a mind maze, and the spiral is so strong that even when you do receive praise, it's too late to see your way out of it.

To counteract the villainous hold, shift your focus away from seeking approval from others and shift inward toward self-praise and recognition. This is done using the same method others would use to commend you. Understand your value, recognize your strengths, and commend your aspirations. When you do this, it helps in two ways:

1. **Self-Praise:** You're able to give yourself praise and validate your achievements regardless of what others do because you see your forward progress.
2. **Hold Steady:** You're less swayed by the opinions of others because you have a clear understanding of what direction you're moving in. This doesn't mean you disregard feedback or constructive criticism; it means your self-worth isn't determined by them.

When you align your actions with your values, you naturally cultivate a sense of integrity and self-assuredness. The result is a deep, unshakable connection within that can withstand the mind manipulation brought forward by your Inner Critic. You'll no longer rely solely on external validation, taking away the supervillain's superpower to manipulate your thoughts and emotions.

ESCAPING YOUR INNER PRISON

As the clash between your Inner Champion and Inner Critic rages on, the villainous critic relentlessly wields the dark forces of fear as its master weapon. In the throes of conflict, you suddenly find yourself trapped in a prison of your creation. It's here that the superpower of vulnerability emerges—not as a weakness but as your secret weapon for escape.

How did you find yourself imprisoned? Your Inner Critic used its dark magic to trick you, causing you to believe the only way to win approval is to conceal your true self beneath layers of pretense and guarded emotions. Initially, you believed its tales and you did as it instructed. After all, its requests seemed harmless, a minor compromise for peace and approval.

But each unexpressed emotion, every hidden truth, built a wall masterfully crafted by your Inner Critic to separate you from your authentic self. This lack of self-expression left you in an isolated prison you unknowingly created.

The only way to escape: use your superpower of vulnerability. As you sit in the self-created stronghold, trapped by your emotions, necessity sparks your superpower of vulnerability. You find yourself ready to lay your soul bare without fear of judgment. It's in this moment that you pull out your Tablet of Internal Power and begin to write.

This journal becomes a crucible for transformation, where the act of writing serves as both a rebellion against the Inner Critic's suppression and a step toward a genuine connection with your Inner Champion.

Knowing your time is now, you use the following as guides and begin scribing in your Tablet of Internal Power.

Tablet of Internal Power

Safety:
- Where do you feel the most safe? Why?
- Where do you feel the least safe? Why?
- When was the last time you felt safe enough to share an embarrassing story about yourself?
- When was the last time you felt safe enough to share your deepest hopes and dreams with another person?

Connection:
- When was the last time you allowed yourself to be truly close and connected to another person?
- Are there specific experiences or circumstances that keep you from developing intimate relationships?
- Do you tend to lose sight of your authentic self in friendships or relationships? If so, what are three ways you can think of to proactively prevent this?
- Finish this statement: developing a truly connected relationship with another doesn't mean I . . .

Daily Life:
- How can you be more present in your everyday life?
- What is one thing you'd like to incorporate into your day? Why?
- How can you reach out and authentically connect with at least one person every day?
- What are two ways you can express emotion daily that would allow you to feel safe and comfortable?

Embracing vulnerability is not solely about opening yourself to others; it's a profound pact you make with yourself. A treaty to honor your truth, to feel deeply, and to live authentically. It's a declaration that you will not be imprisoned by the silence imposed by the Inner Critic. Instead, you rise, your authenticity empowering your Inner Champion to turn the tables on your inner villain, silencing it in the process.

LEVEL 7 SUPERHERO TRAINING: THE GREAT ESCAPE

 The life scenarios below serve as a training ground to invoke your inner superpowers and break free from your Inner Critic's stronghold, escaping your inner supervillain and its legion of nefarious sidekicks.

The Unexpected Critique

The Trap: During a work review, you receive unexpected criticism from your boss that feels unfounded. Your Inner Critic sends out a call to arms and its cohorts of insecurity, anger, frustration, fear, and embarrassment quickly answer, ready to trap you in an emotional spiral that takes you further and further away from your inner knowing. What do you do?

The Crossroads of Life

The Trap: Facing a pivotal life decision, uncertainty clouds your vision of the future and your true desires. Paralyzed at the crossroads, your Inner Critic seizes the opportunity, creating doubt with whispers of complacency. "Why venture into the unknown? Isn't the familiar path easier?" it taunts. Then, exploiting its superpower of shapeshifting, the Critic transforms into one of your deepest fears—those closest to you casting judgment on any choice you make. It's a tactic designed to hold you prisoner, to deter you from stepping boldly toward your joy. How will you respond?

The Sharing Paradigm

The Trap: After experiencing a personal setback, you hesitate to share your feelings, fearing judgment or pity. Your Inner Critic reminds you of times in your life when you shared how you felt and those around you viewed you differently after. It hides away their sincere desire to make amends afterward or how it made your bonds stronger. It selectively replays the feelings that were present when you shared. What's worse, this supervillain uses its mind manipulation superpower to hide away the memories of those who did listen and support your feelings fully in times of trial, keeping you imprisoned in the dark shadow of loneliness. What is a hero to do when faced with such a treacherous scenario?

Remember to download your free "Superhero Training Guide" at silenceyourinnercritic.com.

8. SELF-CARE FOR SUPERHEROES

In the sprawling universe of heroes and villains, where epic battles rage, the mightiest power a superhero possesses isn't found in their ability to leap over skyscrapers or to harness the energy of the stars; it's in the quieter, yet equally formidable, act of self-care. This crucial practice is the unsung hero of every superhero's arsenal, a foundational pillar that ensures they can fight another day.

Self-care, in the realm of superheroes, is the careful calibration of their powers and their body to avoid burnout. It's what allows them to stay resilient against the onslaught of challenges thrown their way by sinister villains. A superhero's body and mind require regular rejuvenation to be ready for battle at any moment.

Moreover, self-care embodies the profound understanding that to protect their world, a superhero must first ensure their own well-being. It's a testament to the strength found in rest, in the moments of quiet reflection and connection with their core. These practices are what fuel a superhero's resilience, compassion, and determination.

When a hero goes without self-care, they find themselves lost, their powers dimmed by the very darkness they strive to vanquish.

In this darkness, they find self-care is not just a duty to themselves but a critical mission for the greater good, ensuring these heroes can shine their light in a world tormented by shadows.

THE VOYAGE TO SELF-CARE STARTS HERE

If you're a superhero who has struggled with taking time for yourself, where do you even begin? It's a barrier I faced when I jumped off my workaholic hamster wheel. My Inner Critic had trapped me in a cycle of constant doing, and I had no idea how to stop. It sounds wonderful to take time to soak in the tub and sip on some tea, but is that the only thing that self-care entails? Absolutely not!

Consider self-care as a multifaceted voyage, encompassing physical, mental, emotional, and spiritual landscapes. Each terrain offers unique challenges and rewards, inviting you to explore and nurture yourself across these interconnected vistas.

- **Physical Self-Care:** This is where your journey begins, tending to your body—the vessel that carries you through every battle against stress and fatigue. Physical self-care goes beyond mere relaxation; it's about honoring your body's needs through exercise, nutrition, and rest, ensuring you're equipped for the ongoing duel with daily demands.
- **Mental Self-Care:** Venturing into the mind's labyrinth, mental self-care involves safeguarding your thoughts and fostering a mindset that supports resilience and growth. It's the strategic planning stage of your self-care quest, where you arm yourself with knowledge, engage in stimulating activities, and practice mindfulness to keep the Inner Critic at bay.
- **Emotional Self-Care:** Here, you confront the heart of your inner world, navigating the tumultuous seas of emotions with compassion and understanding. Emotional self-care is about acknowledging your feelings, allowing yourself to

experience and express them without judgment, and seeking connections that support and uplift you.

- **Spiritual Self-Care:** The final frontier, spiritual self-care, transcends the physical plane, offering a connection to something greater than yourself. Whether through meditation, nature, art, or religious practice, it's about finding meaning, purpose, and a sense of belonging in the universe.

Embarking on the self-care journey requires courage, commitment, and curiosity. It's about exploring these domains, discovering what truly nourishes and fulfills you, and integrating these practices into the tapestry of your daily life. As you traverse this path, remember, the goal isn't to reach a destination but to continually evolve, adapting your self-care rituals to meet the changing landscapes of your life.

FORTIFYING YOUR PHYSICAL FORTRESS

For those who embark on this quest to connect with your inner hero, physical self-care is a key platform upon which other strengths are built. It's the deliberate, intentional act of preserving and enhancing your well-being, ensuring you remain physically well enough to face the forces you encounter. This crucial aspect of self-care encompasses a spectrum of practices, including:

- **Proper Nutrition:** Fueling your body with the foods that maintain your energy and vitality.
- **Regular Exercise:** Keeping your physical form agile and strong, ready for any challenge.
- **Sufficient Rest:** Allowing your body to recover and rejuvenate, ensuring your mind and spirit remain sharp and resilient.
- **Hygiene Practices:** Maintaining cleanliness as a testament to respect and care for your body.

- **Stress Management:** Mastering the art of tranquility amid chaos.
- **Preventive Healthcare:** Staying vigilant against potential threats to your physical health.

By nurturing your physical well-being, you lay the foundation for mental, emotional, and spiritual resilience. This interconnectedness fortifies you, making it harder for the Inner Critic to exploit weaknesses and cast you into doubt.

Physical Self-Care Strategies

To keep your Inner Champion at the height of its powers, consider integrating these strategies into your daily ritual.

1. **Embrace the Power of Rest:** Sleep is when your body heals the most, and every superhero needs time to recover from the day's battles. Do your best to keep a consistent sleep schedule so you can train your body to get quality sleep each night. It's also helpful to establish a fifteen-minute pre-sleep routine before getting into bed, such as listening to calming music as you wash your face and brush your teeth or meditating and journaling. This signals to your body that you're ready to rest. Finally, create a serene environment conducive to deep, restorative sleep.

2. **Nourish to Flourish:** While every hero has different dietary requirements to support their super strength, some things remain constant among all. The bulk of foods consumed should be nutrient-rich, and hydration is a must. Water is crucial for your body for many reasons, but removing toxins is high on that list. Toxin buildup will create brain fog and give your Inner Critic a minefield to play with.

3. **Move with Joy:** Find delight in physical activity—let it be your dance of defiance against the Inner Critic's gloom. Movement releases a cascade of joy hormones, banishing the shadows where the Inner Critic lurks.

4. **Guardianship of Hygiene:** Uphold the rites of cleanliness not as vanity, but as an affirmation of self-respect and a reflection of health. This self-commitment rebuffs the Inner Critic's narrative of neglect.

5. **Recovery as a Ritual:** Listen to your body, honor your physical needs, and seek professional care and support when necessary.

Adapt and personalize these practices to fit your hero's journey, keeping the flames of self-compassion and awareness lit. As your path winds and turns, your self-care strategies may need to adapt. Embrace change as the constant companion of growth. Always keep in mind that your physical self-care isn't mere maintenance; it's your dedication to readiness, resilience, and rebellion against the tyranny of your Inner Critic.

BOLSTERING YOUR MENTAL POWERS

In the ongoing battle between your inner superhero and villain, mental self-care is the superpower that enhances your mental agility, fortifies resilience, and illuminates the path to positivity. It's about sharpening your mind's edge, managing stress with finesse, and fostering a mindset where your Inner Champion thrives while your Inner Critic fades into oblivion.

Acknowledging the significance of mental well-being is like your inner superhero discovering an untapped reservoir of power. This journey toward mental fortification not only boosts cognitive prowess, but also equips you with enhanced problem-solving skills, diminishes anxiety, and nurtures a harmonious balance within. Armed with these capabilities, the shadowy whispers of the Inner Critic lose their grip.

Blueprint for Building Mental Resilience

Mental self-care is the cornerstone of cognitive endurance and creativity, paving the way for continuous personal evolution and the strengthening of your heroic self-relationship.

Here's your arsenal of strategies, blending timeless wisdom with cutting-edge technology, to safeguard your mental domain.

1. **Mastering Mindfulness:** Embrace mindfulness meditation and practices as your allies, anchoring you in the present and fostering a nonjudgmental awareness of your thoughts. These practices enhance relaxation, sharpen focus, and clear the fog of stress.

2. **Seek Mental Stimulation and Inspiration:** Explore creative activities, such as writing, painting, or playing musical instruments, fostering self-expression and mental stimulation. Broaden your perspectives by attending lectures or seminars or exploring different viewpoints through books, podcasts, or documentaries. By stimulating your mind, you're working it out like you would your body with physical exercise.

3. **Mindful Gaming:** If you're a gamer, play video games that incorporate mindfulness techniques. These types of games include calming activities, such as virtual gardening or meditation, within the game environment to reduce stress and promote mental well-being.

4. **Virtual Support Groups:** Find and attend an online community that supports mental well-being. In these types of groups, participants can connect with others facing similar challenges while the organization provides resources and discussion prompts.

5. **Transformational Coaches:** Engage with a coaching platform that provides personalized strategies for improving mental well-being. When finding a coach, I encourage you

to use the *Top 10 Questions to Ask When Interviewing Your "Person in the Chair" (Your Coach)* list that you'll find in the back of this book. Aligning yourself with a transformational coach who supports you on your journey can be a difference-maker.

Keep in mind, if you choose to use any of the technology-based techniques, they're not a replacement for professional mental care. They should be used in conjunction with traditional methods of self-care and seeking professional guidance when needed. With that said, as technology continues to advance, there are exciting opportunities to explore new avenues for mental self-care, and I'm incredibly excited to see where it's taking us.

THE HERO'S SAFEGUARD: EMOTIONAL SELF-CARE

Emotional self-care is the artful practice of tuning into and nurturing your emotional health with intention and mindfulness. It's about becoming adept at recognizing, understanding, and positively responding to the myriad of emotions that color your daily life, turning potential upheavals into triumphs.

This journey begins with distinguishing between emotions and feelings—a nuanced dance between our instinctive responses and the enduring impressions they leave behind. Emotions are the raw, unfiltered reactions to the world around you, and they generally manifest physically in your body. They arise as a quickened pulse in moments of anticipation or a surge of warmth in the heat of anger. These are the primal signals that precede feelings, the deeper, more enduring interpretations shaped by our thoughts and beliefs. It's here, in the space between feeling and emotion, that the Inner Critic seizes its territory and wages war on your emotional state.

But in the arsenal of the mindful hero, emotional self-care serves as protection against such incursions. By cultivating practices that foster emotional resilience and awareness, you fortify your inner defenses, allowing your Inner Champion to emerge victorious, banishing the Inner Critic from the realm of influence.

Strengthening Your Emotional Resilience

Let's dive into a few strategies and techniques to support emotional self-care.

1. **Charting Emotional Territories:** Take time to develop a greater understanding of your emotions and your emotional triggers as they arise, acknowledging and accepting them without judgment. You can do this in healthy ways, such as journaling, talking to a trusted friend, or even using art as an outlet. Once you have taken time to recognize and understand your emotions and your triggers, it becomes much easier to express these triggers, and the emotions tied to them, clearly and concisely.

2. **Exploring Virtual Emotional Realms:** Use virtual reality experiences to immerse yourself in situations that evoke different emotions, helping you understand and manage them better in real life. Giving yourself a safe space to feel the emotional trigger, plus time to explore and navigate through it, can be a very caring act and can prepare you for navigating these situations in daily life.

3. **Emotional Soundscape Creation:** Compose playlists or create your own musical soundscapes that support your various emotional states. This will allow you to nurture your inner world when you find yourself feeling these emotions. For example, you could have a "pick me up" playlist that you use when you are feeling sad, a "good times" playlist for when you're happy and a "heart heal" playlist for when you're experiencing heartbreak.

4. **Mind Mapping Your Emotional Ecosystem:** Create a mind map visualizing each emotion, helping you identify connections and root causes. Once you can see where your emotions are triggering, you can do something about it by making new choices. As you do this, you start to knock your Inner Critic out of the emotional driver's seat. I'll include an example of an emotional mind map and a blank copy you can download at silenceyourinnercritic.com.

5. **Gaming with Emotional Insight:** There are opportunities to pair emotional self-care with interactive games. Using biofeedback technology, you play games while also monitoring your emotional state, helping you learn to regulate and channel your emotions constructively.

In the realm of emotional self-care, the path is uniquely yours to forge. From high-tech adventures to the simple, reflective power of a playlist, the goal is to nurture your emotional well-being in ways that resonate and rejuvenate. As you embark on this journey, remember: your Inner Champion grows stronger with each step, guided by the light of self-awareness and the power of self-care.

EMPOWERING YOUR SPIRIT

The strength of spirit is a beacon that guides heroes through the darkness, a sanctuary from the storms wrought by villains and inner turmoil alike. Spiritual self-care is the sacred practice of forging this inner sanctum, a journey to align with your core essence and beliefs, and a connection to the universal tapestry.

As you continue further into your hero's journey, this spiritual odyssey invites you to delve into the depths of your being, to explore the values, purpose, and profound bonds that link you to the fabric of the universe itself. It's a quest for meaning that transcends the physical, enriching your existence with a sense of belonging and understanding that uplifts and sustains through the many trials that lay ahead.

Building Your Spiritual Sanctum Sanctorum

The path of spirituality is uniquely yours, a reflection of your innermost yearnings and truths. Here are the keystones for building your spiritual resilience.

- **Prayer and Meditation:** Harness these ancient practices to anchor your spirit in the present, connecting deeply with the essence of your being. Let each breath be a prayer, each moment of stillness a meditation on your place within the universe.

- **Connecting with Nature:** Take time to witness and appreciate the role of nature in spiritual practices, finding solace, awe, and connection to your natural environment. Engage in activities that allow you to deeply connect with nature, such as hiking, gardening, or simply spending quiet moments sitting in natural settings, allowing yourself to embrace nature in new ways.

- **Fellowship of Spirits:** Engage and connect with communities that both align with and differ from your spiritual beliefs, providing opportunities to learn from one another and uplift each other. Utilize love as the thread that binds you, fostering a sense of belonging, connection, and collective spirituality.

- **Engaging in Acts of Service and Kindness:** Embody your spiritual values through kindness and service. Each act of compassion is a ripple in the pond of the universe, a testament to the interconnectedness of all souls, and a reinforcement of your spiritual integrity.

- **Wisdom of the Ages:** Immerse yourself in the spiritual teachings that have guided humanity across centuries.

> From ancient texts to modern musings, find the universal truths that resonate with your soul, allowing them to illuminate your path and inspire your actions.

Spiritual self-care serves as the beacon that guides you, connecting you to your deeper purpose. It offers a sense of belonging and perspective, illuminating your path and empowering you to transcend the Inner Critic's myopic vision, reminding you of the larger journey at hand. As you weave these practices into the fabric of your daily life, your journey becomes an epic tale of discovery, growth, and transcendence—a true hero's saga.

THE NEVER-ENDING BATTLE

In the grand narrative of your life, you are the protagonist, the hero of your epic tale, embarking on a journey fraught with challenges, adversaries, and growth. Central to this adventure is the continuous battle with a formidable foe, the Inner Critic, a villain adept at exploiting vulnerabilities and casting shadows of doubt across your path. To stand resilient against this pervasive adversary, your inner hero must embrace a holistic self-care routine, a multifaceted strategy that fortifies every aspect of your being: physical, mental, emotional, and spiritual.

Physical Self-Care is the foundational armor, ensuring your body is strong, energized, and ready for action.

Mental Self-Care sharpens your strategic mind, honing your hero's wit and wisdom—a vital skill for outmaneuvering your foe.

Emotional Self-Care is the shield guarding your heart, allowing you to navigate your emotions with grace and resilience. This keeps the Inner Critic from using your emotions against you.

Spiritual Self-Care is the beacon that guides you, connecting you to your deeper purpose and the universe itself.

Together, these practices weave a hero's tale of strength and resilience, enabling you to meet your Inner Critic head-on with confidence and poise. They remind you that self-care is not a solitary act but a communal one, shared with fellow heroes navigating their stories. As you tend to your holistic well-being, you not only prepare yourself for the battles within, but also support and inspire those around you, collectively strengthening your resolve against the shadows that seek to diminish your light.

Though the epic saga with our Inner Critic may never fully come to an end, maintaining a balanced self-care routine equips you with the tools, strength, and wisdom to face each encounter, grow stronger from it, and make skirmishes shorter each time. Through consistent self-care, you ensure that you are always ready, always resilient, and an eternally hopeful champion of your story. You are the guardian of your inner peace.

LEVEL 8 SUPERHERO TRAINING: POWER-UP

 You've navigated intense training, built your superhero armor, and faced battle. Now it's time to recharge so you can fight another day.

The Dawn Patrol: Physical Self-Care

Your Mission: As the city sleeps, you, the vigilant guardian, know the importance of starting the day with strength and agility. Your mission: a sunrise workout that not only tones the body but also sharpens the mind for the battles ahead. Whether it's a brisk morning walk through the metropolis or practicing tai chi in the quiet of your sanctuary, you understand that physical readiness is key to outmaneuvering the shadowy whispers of the Inner Critic. Record your weekly routine.

The Puzzle Box: Mental Self-Care

Your Mission: In your quest to outwit the nefarious schemes of your arch-nemesis, you come across an ancient puzzle box, said to contain the wisdom of the ages. The box has the following letters, all mixed up in a random order. It is said these letters come together to make a sentence of profound knowledge. It is up to you to solve it.

eb rheew oyu rae whiersteo uyo lilw sism oruy flie

What does it mean? (The answer can be found at the bottom of the page.)[1]

The Emotional Compass: Emotional Self-Care

Your Mission: Amid the chaos of your inner world, you find a few minutes of solitude to consult your Emotional Compass. This powerful artifact helps you navigate through the tumultuous seas of emotions, recognizing and accepting them without judgment. You look at this compass and find that it's spinning feverishly, indicating something is out of alignment. Take a moment to feel into your emotions, giving yourself time to understand what arises. Don't hide anything from yourself. As you allow these emotions to flow, write them down.

The Soul Shield: Spiritual Self-Care

Your Mission: In the epic battle against the forces of doubt and negativity in your mind, you have the sacred power to invoke your Soul Shield. This powerful, luminous barrier protects and strengthens your spirit, giving you unparalleled strength. Each day, as you rise, you'll begin by reinforcing this shield through moments of meditation, envisioning a radiant light that surrounds and fortifies your inner being. With each breath, you bring sacred energy through your body, grounding yourself into the earth's strength and connecting you with the divine power that guides you. As you move through your day, you use mindful moments of gratitude to

---

1   Be where you are, otherwise you will miss your life.

serve as quick power-ups, replenishing your shield and ensuring it remains strong. As night falls, you intentionally breathe in peace and breathe out all stress of the day, restoring your spiritual armor as you prepare for the next day. Your Soul Shield is crafted through intentional care and unwavering focus, protecting the hero within on your journey to self-empowerment.

* Remember to download your free "Superhero Training Guide" at silenceyourinnercritic.com.

9. BOUNDARY LINES
ARE DRAWN

As the frequency of confrontations between you and the shadowy Inner Critic begins to wane, the establishing of firm boundary lines is a crucial next step, serving as demarcation lines for your personal domain. These boundaries clearly mark the sacred grounds of your soul city, delineating what is acceptable and what breaches the peace of your inner sanctuary.

Personal boundaries serve as a warning to the Inner Critic and its eerie entourage, signaling that their tactics of undermining and intrusion will find no entry. Moreover, these boundary lines communicate to the inhabitants of your external world—friends, foes, and allies alike—the terms of engagement with your spirit, ensuring respect, understanding, and mutual support. By setting these boundaries, you reinforce the sovereignty of your inner landscape, safeguarding your physical, emotional, and mental well-being. It's a declaration of your values, limits, and needs, inviting only those interactions that nourish and uplift you while warding off the forces that seek to destabilize and diminish your powers.

In the narrative of your heroic journey, the crafting of boundaries is not a one-time event but an evolving process reflective of your growth, discoveries, and shifts in the dynamic landscape of your life. Each boundary set is a victory, a reinforcement of your resilience, and a step toward the ultimate triumph of your Inner Champion.

CREATING AN IMPENETRABLE FORCE FIELD

Personal boundaries serve as the fortress walls that safeguard your autonomy, outlining the sovereign territory of your being. These barriers, invisible yet as formidable as any superhero's defense mechanism, are vital in delineating the space where your will prevails, setting strict protocols for how others may approach and interact with you.

The world, with its unpredictable storms and challenges, often launches assaults that test your superpower of resilience, creating openings for the Inner Critic to unleash its villainous influence. This shadowy adversary thrives in moments of confusion and uncertainty, exploiting your bafflement to weaken your resolve. In these times, your personal boundaries morph into an impenetrable force field, a dynamic defense system calibrated to your core values and convictions, repelling the advances of negativity and self-doubt.

Erecting this fortress requires a deep understanding of your worth and a commitment to self-respect. It's about establishing clear protocols for emotional exchange, safeguarding your energy, and protecting the sanctity of your mental and emotional well-being. Through these boundaries, you communicate to the world—and to the Inner Critic lurking within—that you are the master of your realm and the architect of your destiny, and that you will not be swayed by external forces or internal sabotage.

These boundaries do more than merely protect; they affirm your place in the world as a hero of value, deserving of respect and autonomy. They allow you to interact with confidence, engaging with others from a position of strength and mutual respect. In crafting these shields around your psyche, you not only neutralize the threat of the Inner Critic, but also create a sanctuary where your true self can thrive.

BEING A SUPERHERO IS NOT ONE-SIDED

Embracing the mantle of heroism demands more than donning a cape and standing tall against adversity; it requires a deep, introspective journey into the essence of who you aspire to be and how you desire to show up in the world. A true superhero steps forth into the day not only aware of the boundaries that safeguard their essence, but also fully aware of the responsibility their actions and interactions carry. Beware, for without this balance, there's a fine line between being celebrated as a defender of justice and inadvertently donning the cloak of the villain.

Guiding principles consciously craft the contours of your life's journey, helping you transition from being a passive participant in life to becoming the hero of your destiny—a future that echoes with the positivity and self-realization that dismantles the nefarious labyrinth constructed by your Inner Critic.

In this grand adventure of heroism, power lies in the combination of setting boundaries and embracing accountability with grace. This power-packed combination ensures that as you wield your powers for the greater good, you remain vigilant against the shadows within that might lead you astray. It's in this dance between integrity and action that the true hero is forged.

SETTING YOUR BOUNDARIES AND PRINCIPLES

It's time to begin the sacred rite of establishing your boundaries and guiding principles. To unlock this power, let's embark on a journey of visualization. Picture yourself in the heart of a boundless expanse, armed with nothing but a piece of chalk and the vastness of the stone beneath your feet as your canvas. With a steady hand, you trace a circle around yourself, its size dictated solely by your intuition. This circle symbolizes the personal space you deem necessary for your well-being.

Visualize this space clearly. This circle, your sanctuary, is safeguarded by the boundaries and principles you set. Every time you permit someone or something to breach your boundaries, you're inviting them into this sacred circle, reducing the space meant solely for you. Reflect on the balance you seek; how many crossings can your sanctuary endure before it becomes too congested, leaving you feeling tormented?

Similarly, whenever you stray from your guiding principles, the core values that define your essence, you step beyond your sacred circle. Question how often you can wander before your sanctuary fades from view, lost to the horizon.

Know that as you evolve and grow in your hero's journey, so, too, will your understanding of yourself, prompting your circle to move, shift, and change. This is natural and expected. However, there's a profound difference between intentional growth and losing yourself to the desires of others or societal expectations. Diluting your essence by continuously stepping out of your circle or over-crowding it with unwelcome influences can distance you from your true hero's nature, making the journey back to authenticity a formidable challenge.

Deciphering Your Hero's Code

Sometimes the challenge of knowing where to begin in identifying your needs is more overwhelming than facing down the most treacherous supervillain. If you're like me in this regard, let me offer you a few prompts and questions to help identify your core values, desires, and needs, empowering you to establish boundaries and guiding principles that align with your authentic self.

As you embark on this exercise, take a moment to clearly pinpoint what truly matters most to you. Assess how you will prioritize and reinforce these essential aspects in your life. With this understanding, you'll possess the vital components necessary to sculpt personal boundaries and guiding principles. These tools will serve as empowering standards that bolster your Inner Champion. Through this process, you'll gain clarity on your core values, transforming them into actionable guides that lead to a more authentic and empowered existence.

Core Values

1. What beliefs are of the greatest importance to you in life?
2. What qualities do you admire most in others?
3. What causes or issues do you feel most passionate about?
4. What ethical guidelines steer your decision-making?
5. What character strengths do you possess that make you feel empowered?
6. What type of an impact do you desire to make on the world?
7. Which activities make you feel most aligned with your authentic self?
8. When do you feel most proud of who you are and what you stand for?
9. What are your non-negotiables in everyday life?
10. What are the cornerstones of your personal philosophy?

Core Desires

1. What experiences make you feel genuinely happy and fulfilled?
2. If you could have any career, what would it be and why?
3. What relationships or connections do you crave most deeply and why?
4. What activities or hobbies ignite your passion and enthusiasm?
5. If you could live anywhere, where would it be, and what draws you there?
6. What type of lifestyle aligns with your heart's desires?
7. What moments or achievements would make you feel profoundly content?

8. What do you wish to contribute to the world?
9. What personal goals or dreams inspire you to act?
10. When do you feel most in tune with your innermost desires?

Core Needs

1. What emotional conditions are necessary for your well-being?
2. What intellectual or mental stimulation do you require?
3. What physical aspects of your life contribute to your sense of balance?
4. What type of social interactions and connections are vital to you?
5. When do you feel the most secure and safe?
6. What level of autonomy and independence do you need?
7. What type of support or recognition fuels your motivation?
8. How much downtime or solitude is essential for your mental health?
9. What is non-negotiable for you in your relationships?
10. When do you feel the most comfortable and at ease in your own skin?

Boundaries Unleashed: Crafting Your Hero's Code

When writing your boundaries, it's important that you're as clear and specific as possible. This will ensure that everyone who hears them can understand and adhere to them, including you.

As you create your personal boundaries, here are a few helpful tips.

- Use "I" statements to make them self-focused.
- Create them in the present tense, allowing you and others to know they are being enforced now.
- Clearly define the purpose of the boundary so there's no confusion when sharing them with others.

- Establish consequences for boundary violations; otherwise, there's no reason for someone to honor them.

I'm going to share a few of my personal boundaries and guiding principles with you to serve as examples. I'm not claiming mine are the ideal standard. I'd offer there's no such thing as an ideal standard with something this personal. I'm simply hopeful my boundaries can serve as a template for you to build your own.

Personal Boundary Examples

1. I am valuable and only allow myself to be treated with kindness, love, and respect. If I feel I am being treated in any other way—physically, mentally, emotionally, or spiritually—I remove myself immediately.
   - This boundary has the "I" statement.
   - It's in the present tense.
   - It's clear that the purpose is to know and hold to my value.
   - The consequence is that I will leave if my boundary is violated.
2. My time and space are equally as valuable as those of the people around me. I only allow them to be used in ways I have agreed to. If I discover that my time or my space is being taken or used in a way that does not align with me, I stop immediately and do not re-engage until I have a clear understanding of the purpose.
   - The boundary is self-focused.
   - It's present tense.
   - The purpose is to create a boundary around how my time is valued and used.
   - The consequence is set for the action I will take if a violation occurs (stop and not re-engage until I understand).

3. I say no when I mean no and yes when I mean yes, and I do not accept external pressure, including guilt or shame, for my response. If I feel someone is pressuring me, I am empowered to kindly disengage from the conversation or ignore the pressure and hold to my decision.
   - This is an "I" statement boundary.
   - It's set in the present tense.
   - The purpose is to clearly remove the pressure and guilt that my Inner Critic shares or that I receive from others for my choices.
   - The consequence is that I will disengage or ignore.

Scribing the Principles of Your Inner Hero

Using your Hero's Code from above, record your guiding principles to serve as your personal superhero's code of conduct. Staying with the same approach as you did above with your boundaries, keep your guiding principles:

- "I statement" focused;
- Present tense;
- And clear and concise.

Guiding Principles Examples

1. I am grateful for the blessings in my life, but I also ask, "What else is possible?"
2. I look for strengths in others and the positive in every situation.
3. I take risks and embrace the outcome.
4. I show compassion for myself and others.
5. I believe in myself and trust what I know to be true for me.

There isn't a maximum number of guiding principles you're out to achieve when creating your lists. You may also find that once you've created your list, you recognize new ones as the weeks progress. Feel free to add to your creation, moving things around and removing things as needed. Both your boundaries and your guiding principles will be a living document.

Mobilizing Your Heroic Code

With your tablets of boundaries and principles meticulously forged in the crucible of self-reflection, the next crucial step is deployment into the field of battle. Enshrine them not just in the sanctum of your mind, but in the world around you, transforming them from ideals into invincible armaments. Establish these guiding pillars into tangible reminders, standing tall in your everyday environment where they can serve as constant beacons, marking the path of the hero you've vowed to embody.

Consider these steps to ensure your heroic code is always within arm's reach.

- **Deploy Post-It Note Beacons:** Scatter these colorful heralds of your inner ethos throughout your lair (home) and command center (office), turning every glance into a moment of empowerment.
- **Summon Digital Familiars:** Program your trusty sidekick (your phone) with reminders that periodically echo your guiding principles, ensuring your focus remains sharp and your resolve unwavering.
- **Carry Your Scroll of Virtues:** Keep a compact version of your code, both your boundaries and principles, within your personal effects (purse or wallet), allowing you to consult it in times of uncertainty or challenge.
- **Proclaim Your Creed:** For those heroes who tread the path of openness, sharing your code on the digital town square (social media) can not only affirm your commitment but inspire fellow travelers on their journey.

Choose the methods that resonate with your heroic spirit, ensuring these codes serve not as mere decorations but as vital, living components of your daily quest. Let each acknowledgment of your hero's creed and boundary lines be a conscious reaffirmation of your path, a mindful meditation on the hero you are and aspire to become. In this way, your principles and boundaries transcend the story and are woven into the very fabric of your reality. They guide your real-life hero's narrative as you navigate the myriad of challenges and adventures that lie ahead.

DEFENDING YOUR HEROIC LIMITS: IDENTIFYING AND COUNTERING BOUNDARY BREACHES

In the chronicle of self-discovery, recognizing when the unwarranted forces breach the barricades of your boundaries is a formidable challenge. This is especially true if years or lifetimes of conditioning have blurred the lines of acceptable behavior. Below is a list of subtle boundary violation signals. This list can help you identify subtle infringements that may otherwise go unnoticed.

Signs of Boundary Violations

1. **Discomfort Signals:** Feeling uncomfortable, angry, or resentful around a particular person or situation each time you encounter them is often a sign that your boundaries are being crossed. This does not mean that the person or situation is bad and should be condemned. It means that there's cause to understand where lines are being crossed or unenforced.

2. **Energy Siphon:** If you frequently feel emotionally or physically drained after interacting with someone, it may indicate that they are not respecting your boundaries. This is a sign to investigate where your boundaries are not clearly understood or enforced.

3. **Self-Neglect:** If you consistently prioritize someone else's needs and neglect your own, it may be a sign there's an opportunity for a boundary to be set and enforced by you.

4. **Feeling Pressured:** Feeling pressured to do things you don't desire to do, or saying yes when you want to say no, suggests you're not holding to boundaries you've set or that your boundaries are not being respected.

5. **Defensive Rationale:** If you find yourself constantly justifying your decisions or overexplaining your boundaries, it's a prime indicator that your boundaries are not being received or listened to.

6. **Unwelcome Contact:** Any form of non-consensual physical interaction is an outright boundary violation and should be stopped immediately.

7. **Manipulation or Guilt-Tripping:** People who manipulate or guilt-trip you into doing things you're not comfortable with are traversing your boundaries, knowingly or unknowingly.

8. **Constant Criticism:** Continuous criticism, especially if you've established a boundary in the area being criticized, is an infringement.

9. **Ignoring Your Wishes:** When others consistently disregard and ignore your wishes, whether it's by taking your time, invading your personal space, or ignoring your emotional needs, this is an indication of boundary violations.

10. **Privacy Invasion:** If someone invades your privacy, such as going through your personal belongings or personal information without your consent, it can be a significant breach of your boundaries.

Recognizing these signals arms you with the awareness needed to uphold your heroic barriers.

Tactics for Boundary Reinforcement

Once you've discovered your boundaries have been breached, your mission becomes clear: to reinforce your sacred spaces with clarity and compassion. Let's explore the superhero tools and tactics you have at your disposal.

1. **Inner Sentinel Activation:** Using your superpower of self-awareness, take time to reflect on your feelings around the boundary. Understand the specifics around the violation and why it made you uncomfortable. Is there a need to act?

2. **Strategic Pause Module:** Before engaging, activate your power of pause to recalibrate your emotional and mental energies. This ensures you respond with calm precision rather than reactive force.

3. **The Great Communicator:** Deploy clear, assertive communication of your boundaries, even if the individual has already been made aware of them. Use "I" statements to describe your feelings and needs. For example, say, "I feel uncomfortable when . . ." or "I need . . . "

4. **Consequence Configuration:** Communicate the consequences of further boundary violations. Let the person know what will happen if the behavior continues. Be prepared to follow through with these consequences; otherwise, people will believe that your consequences are empty threats.

5. **Nonverbal Defense Array:** Utilize the silent strength of body language to underscore your boundaries. These nonverbal cues could include stepping back to show distance or putting your hand, palm facing out, in front of your chest to signal discomfort with social proximity.

6. **Consistently Enforced Boundaries:** Regularly enforce your boundaries. This constant upholding serves as both

a reminder to yourself of your worth and a clear signal to others of your serious commitment.

7. **Archival System:** Maintain detailed records of transgressions, particularly if they form a pattern. This log serves as both a personal reminder and, if necessary, evidence in seeking support or resolution.

8. **Containment Protocol:** In cases of severe or relentless boundary violations, it may become necessary to create distance or sever ties, preserving your mental and emotional fortress. This drastic measure, while a last resort, is sometimes essential for your well-being.

9. **Regenerative Care:** Following a confrontation, initiate self-care protocols to rejuvenate your spirit. This might include engaging in activities that restore your inner peace and strength.

Asserting your boundaries is essential for your protection and efficacy in the ongoing quest for peace and personal integrity. Though the path may challenge your resolve, remember it's in upholding your boundaries that you reclaim your power, define your true self, and ensure your saga is one of triumph.

THE POWER OF POSITIVE COMMUNICATION

Navigating interpersonal dynamics demands more than setting up your supercharged boundary defenses; it also requires the mastery of open, honest communication. Letting your boundaries morph into unspoken expectations is similar to handing your nemesis, the Inner Critic, a secret weapon. The villain suddenly has the power to transform your thoughts and feelings around your boundaries into expectations, and then trigger anger when those expectations aren't met. The antidote? Crystal-clear communication of your superhero code.

Without the mystical ability to read minds, your fellow citizens and allies are left in the dark about your boundary lines. It's your duty, as a diligent guardian of your inner sanctum, to articulate these lines clearly. Imagine, for a moment, the strength required to reveal your core principles to allies and adversaries alike, stating, "Here's what I stand for, and here's how I safeguard my peace." This act of bravery not only fortifies your defenses, but also invites those who respect your values to stand with you.

The pathway to fostering robust and positive connections begins within your sacred chamber of self-reflection. Once you've engaged in an honest dialogue with yourself, identifying your true needs and desires, you're ready to broadcast these signals to the world. Here's your tactical communication guide to ensure your messages are not only sent but are received and respected.

- **Initiate the Self-Scout Protocol**: Understand your boundaries thoroughly before engaging in discussions. Clarity is your ally.
- **Deploy "I" Beacons:** Use "I" statements as signals of your experiences and feelings, avoiding the alienating effect of blame.
- **Precision Targeting:** Be as specific as a laser-guided system when conveying what you need or desire. Ambiguity is the enemy of understanding.
- **Optimal Timing Detection:** Identify calm moments for discussions, avoiding the chaos of conflict or distraction.
- **Activate Dual Receivers:** Engage in active listening after you've shared your message. Dialogue is a two-way communication stream.
- **Nonverbal Communication Array:** Your body language, vocal tone, and expressions are powerful communicators. Ensure they're aligned with your message.
- **Assertiveness Over Aggression:** Assertiveness is about expressing your boundaries with confidence and respect, while aggression involves hostility or disrespect. Strive to be assertive in your communication.

- **Adaptability to Communication Frequencies:** Tune into the preferred communication styles of your audience for maximum effectiveness.
- **Endurance Mode:** Patience is a virtue when navigating complex dialogues. Stay committed to the process.
- **Gratitude Signal:** Acknowledge those who honor your boundaries with gratitude, reinforcing positive interactions and alliances.

Effective communication is a super skill that improves with practice. By applying these tips and being mindful of your communication style, you can enhance your ability to express your needs and desires in a healthy and productive way.

NAVIGATING BOUNDARIES IN THE RELATIONSHIP MAZE

The maze of relationships is diverse and intricate. As the hero of your life, understanding the unique puzzle of each relationship is crucial when sketching the boundaries of your inner realm. The parameters you deploy in the workplace, for instance, are vastly different from those you draw around the sanctuaries shared with your inner circle of family and friends. This adaptability is your cloak, allowing you to move fluidly through the various domains of your life.

Consider your boundaries as a flexible force field, although impenetrable it is capable of reshaping and resizing based on your environment and adjusting as the dynamics of your relationships evolve. Your journey through life is one of continual transformation—your alliances, your environments, and you, yourself, are in a state of perpetual motion. It's imperative, then, to regularly recalibrate your boundaries, ensuring they remain in harmony with your current chapter, environment, and the characters within it.

Embrace the fluidity of these boundary lines, acknowledging that flexibility does not mean weakness; rather, it's a testament to your strength, awareness, and adaptability as the protagonist of your story. By regularly evaluating and adjusting your boundaries, you ensure they serve not as barriers to enjoying your life, but as lines in the sand, navigating you through the rich tapestry of the relationships that shape your world.

LEVEL 9 SUPERHERO TRAINING: MIGHTY DEFLECTION

In this chapter, you've embarked on a crucial mission: drafting your Superhero Code—a comprehensive compilation of personal boundaries and guiding principles that define your path and protect your essence against the villainous Inner Critic and its legion. This Code is not only your shield, but also a guide to help you through the intricate maze of relationships and self-discovery.

The Villain's Monologue

Write a monologue from the perspective of your Inner Critic, detailing how it plans to breach your newly established boundaries. Then, script a heroic retort from your Inner Champion, reinforcing your boundaries and demonstrating your resilience. This exercise will prepare you for real-life encounters with your Inner Critic.

The Boundary Simulation

Imagine three different scenarios where your boundaries are tested; these could involve work, family, or social situations. For each scenario, write down a step-by-step action plan for how you'll reinforce your boundaries, employing the tactics of clear communication, assertiveness, and self-care. Role-playing these scenarios mentally prepares you to handle real-life situations with confidence.

The Guiding Principles Manifesto

Create a vibrant poster or digital wallpaper that lists your top five guiding principles. Use bold fonts and colors that resonate with you. This visual reminder will serve as a daily inspiration, motivating you to live in alignment with your core values.

* Remember to download your free "Superhero Training Guide" at silenceyourinnercritic.com.

10. A LIFE OF TRIUMPH

Although your Inner Champion will never fully defeat your Inner Critic, your hero within now has the power to silence this villain whenever it might surface. As this supervillain wages its attacks on your thoughts, you're powerful enough to quickly redirect and reshape them. Through these new thoughts, you're now writing the story of your life that you desire.

LIFE AFTER YOU'VE SILENCED YOUR INNER CRITIC

Armed with the superpowers you've unearthed, the comprehensive arsenal you've amassed, the protective armor you've forged, and the rigorous training you've embraced, you've successfully reclaimed the realm of your inner world, including the dominion of your thoughts.

The narrative of your life, once overshadowed by the Inner Critic's tyranny, is now yours to tell. You've wrested back the pen and, with it, the power to script your destiny in the ink of your own making.

SWEEPING THE STREETS OF YOUR INNER METROPOLIS

Once you've freed the streets of your inner cityscape from the stronghold of your Inner Critic, you must remain vigilant.

Like any seasoned supervillain, the Inner Critic lurks in the shadows, biding its time as it waits for you to let your defenses down so it can strike once again. Maintain a vigilant patrol along the pathways of your life, making certain you're taking conscious and consistent steps to keep your inner realm safe and secure.

Here are several engaging strategies to keep watch over your inner metropolis.

- **Playful Exploration:** Embrace life with a childlike sense of wonder and curiosity. Explore your surroundings with fresh eyes, like you're seeing everything for the first time. Engage in activities like painting, dancing, or playing a musical instrument without any concern for perfection. Allow playfulness to spark your creativity and joy.
- **Extreme Empathy:** Cultivate deep empathy by seeking to understand the perspectives and emotions of those with whom you disagree or who have wronged you. This practice can help dissolve bitterness and pave the way for empathy and forgiveness.
- **Journaling from Different Perspectives:** Write in a journal from the perspective of your ideal self, a fictional character, or even an inanimate object. This technique allows you to gain insights and solutions from different angles, fostering creativity and problem-solving.
- **Nature Immersion:** Spend time in nature without distractions. Practice forest bathing, which involves immersing yourself in a natural environment and mindfully connecting with the sights, sounds, and sensations around you. Nature can inspire awe and tranquility.
- **Random Acts of Kindness for Yourself:** Show yourself unexpected kindness. Extend to yourself the same level of

compassion and care that you would during a Random Acts of Kindness event.

- **Metaphorical Thinking**: Use metaphors to reframe challenges. For example, if you're facing a difficult decision, imagine it as a crossroads in a magical forest, where each path leads to a unique adventure. Metaphorical thinking can make complex situations feel more manageable.

- **Personify Your Fear:** If you're struggling with fear or self-doubt, give these emotions a persona or personality. Imagine them as characters in your story and engage in conversations with them, as I have throughout this book with the Inner Critic. This technique can help you understand and disarm your fears.

- **Storytelling Meditation:** Craft a positive and empowering narrative about your life. Imagine your life as a storybook or movie, with you as the resilient hero facing challenges and growing through them. Use this narrative to inspire and motivate yourself.

These unconventional techniques give you fun ways to keep guard over your life story with fresh perspectives. This is your life. Continue to be the hero of your story and write the narrative the way you desire it to unfold.

LEVEL 10 SUPERHERO TRAINING: INNER CITY WATCH

Having liberated your inner landscape, the task now is to ensure it remains free from the villainous Inner Critic's return. This chapter focused on proactive measures to patrol your inner realm, engaging with your environment creatively, to sustain the hard-won peace that you've achieved. It's time to put this training into action.

Heroic Reflections

Peace Practice: Start each morning with a five-minute meditation focusing on a personal attribute you appreciate about yourself. This daily reflection helps strengthen your Inner Champion, keeping the Inner Critic at bay.

Empathy Patrol

Peace Practice: Schedule a weekly "empathy walk," where you spend time in a public place, like a park, and consciously attempt to understand the emotions and actions of those around you. This practice not only enhances your empathy, but also helps diffuse any judgment or negativity from others that might trigger your Inner Critic.

Journal of Justice

Peace Practice: Keep a "journal of justice," where you document instances when you successfully maintained boundaries or positively handled interactions that previously would have triggered your Inner Critic. Review this journal monthly to remind yourself of your growth and resilience.

Nature's Ally

Peace Practice: Commit to a bi-weekly "hero's walk" in nature. Use this time to reconnect with the earth and your inner peace, drawing strength from the tranquil setting to fortify your mental and emotional defenses.

Kindhearted Acts of Care

Peace Practice: Challenge yourself to perform at least one random act of kindness for yourself each week. It could be treating yourself to a favorite meal, taking an unplanned day off for rest, or buying yourself a small gift. This nurtures self-love and wards off negative self-talk.

* Remember to download your free "Superhero Training Guide" at silenceyourinnercritic.com.

11. HERO'S QUEST FOR KNOWLEDGE

In the narrative of many superhero stories, the sage mentor can frequently be heard proclaiming to the budding hero, "The student has now become the master." However, this "gal in the chair" sees it very differently. In the vast universe of life's adventures, adopting the stance of a perpetual student is the real superpower. True heroes recognize that mastery is not a final state but an ongoing journey of discovery.

Embrace the role of an eternal learner, open to the endless possibilities that each new lesson holds. Shed the notion that expertise in a field means the end of growth. Even with degrees and decades of experience, there's immense value in viewing knowledge as an ever-expanding horizon. This mindset allows you to transcend the familiar and explore new territories of understanding.

Share your wisdom and insights generously—the world enriches when knowledge flows freely. Yet, let this exchange be a gateway, not a barrier. Let every interaction be an opportunity to learn, to expand beyond the known, and to weave new threads of understanding into the tapestry of your life's journey. As a hero dedicated to lifelong learning, you are not simply absorbing information; you are actively engaging in the evolution of your story and the stories around you.

THE VALOR OF CONTINUOUS LEARNING

In the endless battle against the Inner Critic's weapon of personal stagnation, adopting a mindset of continuous learning equips you with the agility and strength to evolve ceaselessly. This commitment to perpetual growth is not simply an educational pursuit; it fuels your superpowers as it simultaneously dismantles the weapon of inactivity used against you by the villainous Inner Critic.

Key Benefits of Embracing Continuous Learning

- **Heroic Evolution:** Just as superheroes evolve to face new threats, embracing continuous learning allows you to grow and adapt, constantly refining your powers and understanding of the world. This journey transforms you into the best version of yourself, ever ready to meet life's challenges.

- **Resilience Reinforcement:** Each new skill and piece of knowledge you acquire is like adding a piece of armor or a new tool to your armory. This arsenal prepares you to effectively navigate life's tumultuous battles, enhancing your ability to recover from setbacks with agility and grace.

- **Increased Self-Awareness:** Delving into the depths of your mind and soul, continuous learning fosters a profound understanding of your true self. This introspection illuminates your core values and aspirations, strengthening your resolve and relationship with yourself.

- **Empowerment:** Armed with knowledge and skills, you seize the reins of your destiny. This empowerment encourages you to pursue your goals with conviction, actively shaping the narrative of your life.

- **Adaptability:** In a world that shifts like the scenes of a graphic novel, your ability to adapt is crucial. Continuous learning keeps you flexible and ready to face new challenges, turning potential fears into fuel for growth.
- **Enriched Connections:** As you expand your horizons, you also enhance your relationships. Your growth makes you a beacon for others, attracting and inspiring companions who are drawn to your journey.
- **Sense of Fulfillment:** The quest for personal growth generally leads to profound satisfaction and purpose. Knowing your actions contribute positively to the world around you anchors a deep-seated sense of fulfillment.
- **Eternal Learner:** With a lifelong commitment to learning, your intellectual curiosity never wanes. This zest for knowledge protects you from the complacency that can dim even the brightest hero.

By turning your attention toward becoming a continuous learner, you not only thwart the plots of your Inner Critic and enhance your superpowers, but you also enhance every aspect of your existence. This relentless pursuit of knowledge and self-betterment is what truly defines a hero, ensuring that you remain vigilant and victorious in the complex landscape of life.

VALIANT GOALS FOR LIFELONG LEARNING

In the journey of your heroic life, embracing lifelong learning means setting goals not just for external conquests, but also for the essential journey of self-growth. Craft goals that resonate with your inner values and visions, transforming them into powerful tools against the shadows cast by your Inner Critic. These goals provide clarity and direction, acting as beacons of light guiding you through the darker paths where uncertainty and doubt lurk.

When the sinister whispers of your Inner Critic stir, a clear and personalized goal for learning and growth lets you counter with a resolute, "I know my path, and your doubts have no power here." This clarity shields you from being swayed by the villainous chatter, ensuring you remain steadfast and focused.

Setting meaningful goals does more than keep you on track; they ignite a fire within. Aligned with your deepest values, these goals keep your spirit engaged and relentless in the pursuit of what truly matters to you. They fortify your resolve when facing obstacles, enhancing your productivity and giving rise to profound satisfaction with each milestone reached. Such triumphs bolster your self-confidence, reinforcing your belief in your heroic capabilities and elevating your self-esteem.

Moreover, realistic goals challenge you to venture beyond the safe confines of your comfort zone while still offering a reachable victory. This careful balance wards off the peril of burnout and stress—the favorite tools of your Inner Critic.

Through introspection and the continuous shaping of your goals, you cultivate self-awareness and self-compassion, along with a profound connection to your inner hero. As you advance toward these goals, you deepen your understanding of your strengths, embrace your vulnerabilities, and hone your superpowers, crafting a narrative of growth and resilience that celebrates the journey toward becoming the ultimate version of yourself.

LEVEL 11 SUPERHERO TRAINING: LIFELONG LEARNING

As you don your cape each day, remember the journey of a superhero is never complete. The path of continuous learning is the road to harnessing your full potential. By embracing a lifelong learning mindset, you empower your Inner Champion and equip yourself with the resilience needed to thwart the cunning plots of your Inner Critic before they have a chance to wreak havoc. Continuous learning strengthens your mental agility, enhances your emotional resilience, and deepens your spiritual connections, keeping your heroic spirit nimble and ready for any challenge.

The Curiosity Crusade

Your Objective: Cultivate curiosity by exploring new hobbies, reading different genres, or learning a new skill.

The Mission: Once a month, pick something new that sparks your interest. It could be a book outside your usual reading preference, a new physical activity, or a creative endeavor. Reflect on how this new knowledge expands your worldview.

Empathy Encounter

Your Objective: Develop empathy and understanding by engaging with perspectives that differ from your own.

The Mission: Once a week, engage in a conversation with someone whose views challenge your own. Approach the dialogue with openness, aiming to understand rather than to convince. Journal about the experience and any new insights gained.

Mindful Mentorship

Your Objective: Share your knowledge and learn through teaching.

The Mission: Identify opportunities to mentor someone else, perhaps a colleague, friend, or community member. As you guide them, observe how teaching reinforces your understanding and uncovers areas where you can grow.

Adversity Simulator

Your Objective: Improve problem-solving skills and resilience by tackling complex problems.

The Mission: Engage in activities that simulate challenges, such as strategic games, puzzles, or brain teasers. Reflect on your problem-solving process and resilience in facing these challenges.

Vision Quest

Your Objective: Visualize and plan for future growth.

The Mission: Spend time envisioning where you want your journey of self-improvement to lead. Create a vision board or write a mission statement for your personal and professional life. Use this vision to set short-term and long-term goals.

* *Remember to download your free "Superhero Training Guide" at silenceyourinnercritic.com.*

12. OUR JOURNEY COMES TO AN END

Although our journey together ends for now, your amazing story forges onward. Armed with an armory at your disposal, you stand ready to face down your Inner Critic each time it rises. To give you a quick inventory list, here are ten treasures you hold in your arsenal.

TEN TREASURES IN YOUR ARSENAL

1. **Forge a Strong Self-Alliance:** Building a strong relationship with yourself is the foundation for healthy relationships with others. Prioritize self-care, self-acceptance, and self-love.

2. **Confront and Silence Your Inner Critic:** The Inner Critic can negatively impact self-esteem and self-worth. Recognize its presence and counter its influence.

3. **Champion Self-Awareness:** Detect and dismantle self-limiting beliefs and patterns of negative self-talk, breaking free from their constraints to spur personal growth.

4. **Wield Self-Compassion:** Foster self-compassion by treating yourself with kindness, forgiving your mistakes, and supporting your journey with patience.

5. **Embrace Authenticity:** Embrace authenticity by staying true to your personality, values, and spirit. Let go of the need for external validation and societal pressures.

6. **Comprehensive Self-Care:** Commit to supporting all dimensions of your being—physical, emotional, mental, and spiritual. Prioritize activities that rejuvenate and fulfill you.

7. **Draw Your Boundaries:** Establish and maintain healthy personal boundaries and guiding principles. Learn to assertively say no to protect your needs and uphold your values.

8. **Adopt a Growth Mindset:** Continue learning throughout life. Be open to new ideas, explore diverse interests, and view challenges as opportunities for growth.

9. **Transform Negative Thoughts:** Cultivate a positive and empowering mindset by practicing gratitude, reframing negative thoughts, and surrounding yourself with positivity, including positive people.

10. **Seize the Lifelong Journey:** Remember that personal growth is a lifelong journey. Embrace self-acceptance, celebrate progress, and let go of the need for perfection.

By making these ten treasures part of your regular focus, you're equipped to build a strong and nourishing relationship with yourself and pen the hero's tale you desire for your life.

Remember, you don't need to use every technique in this book right after reading it. Choose two or three to start with, and then, as you've integrated those superpowers, revisit the index and choose two or three more. Go at your pace; this isn't a race.

EMBARKING ON YOUR SUPERHERO'S JOURNEY

As you set forth on this grand adventure, remember to:

Harness the Power of Self-Love: Believe deeply in the virtues of self-love and self-acceptance. Let them be part of your hero's armor. You are worthy of kindness, compassion, and joy. Embrace the strength that comes from loving yourself.

Celebrate Your Unique Powers: Honor your true essence and the unique qualities that make you, you. Your superhero abilities are uniquely yours; celebrate your strengths and understand growth is forged through both triumphs and trials.

Trust in Your Evolution: Change is the only constant in the hero's journey. Trust in your ability to adapt and transform, knowing each challenge is a step toward becoming your ultimate self. The unknown is not to be feared but embraced; it holds the keys to new powers and pathways.

Prioritize Your Well-Being: Commit to self-care as fervently as you would to saving the world. Nurture your mind, body, and spirit with activities that restore and energize you. Self-care is your secret weapon for enduring happiness and resilience.

Cultivate a League of Allies: Surround yourself with positivity and cultivate relationships that lift you higher. Seek out fellow heroes who inspire and empower you, and together, strengthen your collective resolve to overcome any darkness.

Practice Patience and Kindness: The path of personal growth is long and winding. Be patient and gentle with yourself as you traverse it. Celebrate each victory, no matter how small, and remember that the pillars of self-compassion and love are what sustain you through the journey.

Embrace Gratitude: Let gratitude be the light that guides you through dark times. Appreciate the lessons, cherish the journey, and find joy in the richness of your experiences. Gratitude will keep your spirits high and your heart open.

Believe in Your Infinite Potential: You are the master of your destiny. With unyielding courage and indomitable will, trust in your inner strength and potential. Your life is an epic saga awaiting your command.

Start Your Quest: Armed with self-awareness, bolstered by allies, and guided by your light, step bravely into your life's adventure. Embrace your inner superhero and let the journey unfold.

With this hero's codex, you're not just setting out to manage your Inner Critic, you're embarking on a lifelong quest to unleash the most heroic version of yourself.

> "You're much stronger than you think you are. Trust me."
> —Superman, *Man of Steel*

LEVEL 12 SUPERHERO TRAINING: A HERO'S LIFE

As you continue your journey from this point onward, remember that being a superhero doesn't mean being perfect. It means being brave enough to face yourself, to learn and grow, and to strive for betterment each day. You are the author of your superhero story—embrace your power, write boldly, and let your Inner Champion shine. Here are a few exercises you can employ as you continue your journey to remain vigilant in your quest.

Courageous Compassion Conclaves
Exercise: Organize monthly "Courageous Compassion Conclaves" with fellow heroes (friends or support groups who are also working on personal growth). Discuss themes like overcoming personal struggles or practicing self-compassion. Share your insights and support each other's journeys, reinforcing the idea that every hero can benefit from a league of allies.

Resilience Rallies
Exercise: Host quarterly "Resilience Rallies" with yourself or within your support network. Reflect on the challenges you've

faced and overcome in the last few months. Celebrate these victories, no matter how small, and set intentions for continuing to build resilience. Use this time to reinforce the importance of progress over perfection.

Learning League

Exercise: Form or join a "Learning League"—a group dedicated to continuous learning and growth. Each month, choose a new book, documentary, or topic to explore together. Discuss what you've learned and how it can be applied to enhance your self-relationship and weaken your Inner Critic.

True Self Check-Ins

Exercise: Schedule a monthly "True Self Check-In" where you check in with yourself to ensure you are living in alignment with your values. Use a set of questions to guide your audit: Am I being true to myself? Are there areas where I feel I'm wearing a mask? What steps can I take this month to be more authentic?

* Remember to download your free "Superhero Training Guide" at silenceyourinnercritic.com.

CONCLUSION: YOUR HERO'S JOURNEY CONTINUES— ADDITIONAL TOOLS

Finding the right person to serve as your "person in the chair" (your coach) as you navigate your superhero journey is important. This individual will become a confidante for your deepest aspirations and a strategist helping you achieve your goals. To ensure you select a guide who can truly amplify your powers as an Inner Champion, it's essential to conduct thorough interviews. By preparing a consistent set of questions, you can effectively compare the answers from potential candidates, ensuring you choose the perfect Alfred Pennyworth to support your superhero endeavors. This careful selection process will equip you with the right ally to navigate the challenges and victories ahead.

TOP 10 QUESTIONS TO ASK WHEN INTERVIEWING YOUR "PERSON IN THE CHAIR" (YOUR COACH)

Below are ten questions that I highly recommend when interviewing your potential coach.

1. **Skills and Experience:** What skills and experience do you bring that will assist me in all aspects of my life—mental, emotional, physical, and spiritual? As you share these skills, provide me with examples of how they've proven valuable to others who have been coached by you.

    This question will allow you to get a clear view of what skills the potential coach brings to the alliance.

    It will also provide you with real-world scenarios where the skills were successfully applied, allowing you to understand if the coach's approach aligns with the way you learn and navigate life.

    Finally, it will show you if the coach is prepared to support you across all aspects of your life: mental, emotional, physical, and spiritual.

2. **Decision-Making:** If I was struggling with a decision, such as [insert your hypothetical struggle here], how would you help me come to a decision and support me as I acted? This question allows you to see the coach's methodology in action.

    It shows you how comfortable the coach is when it comes to sharing their method.

3. **It's Not Working Out:** If I came to you and told you that I didn't feel our coaching agreement was working out for me, what would you do? Is it possible to cancel?

    By asking this question you have a clear idea of how the coach addresses those moments when a client may desire to retreat into comfort and cancel the contract to avoid a challenge.

    You also have details for how the coach receives feedback: Do they ask clarifying questions, seek to understand how they can support you better, offer a cancellation clause in their contract, and other vital details?

4. **Different Lifestyles:** How will you support me if my lifestyle is different from yours, either because of my faith or

my choices? How do you keep your personal perspectives from bleeding into your coaching?

Many coaches may not be aware of how their perspectives impact their coaching styles. By asking this question, you have an opportunity to discover if the coach you're interviewing is not only aware of this potential, but also has a plan to redirect it if it does occur.

You can also discover if they're open to feedback if you feel their personal perspectives are impacting your coaching.

5. **Tracking Progress:** What process do you use to track the progress of your clients?

   As you set goals together and move toward them, it's important to understand how you'll measure progress and success together.

6. **Providing Feedback:** How do you provide needed feedback for any adjustments that need to be made if you notice they aren't meeting your client's goals?

   When life gets busy and you begin to go off course, it's important to know how the coach will provide you with feedback to course-correct and achieve what you set out to do.

7. **Changing Priorities:** Life is full of surprises and sometimes people and situations change. Tell me about a time when you had to shift your approach midway through to adapt to a client's changing situation.

   Life circumstances can come into play on your road to growth. What you start out focusing on may not be what you need to continue to focus on throughout the term of your contract. This question can help you understand how or if your coach will pivot accordingly.

8. **Keeping Current:** How do you stay current with new developments in technology and coaching methodologies available? Do you feel keeping current is important?

Not every coach will place the same importance on keeping current with technology or methodologies. Some will value experience over new approaches. If new technology and methodologies are important to you, this is a key question to include.

9. **Keeping Motivated:** When I feel unmotivated, what strategies do you use for motivation? Are there certain ones you favor over others?

   Most of us reach points when motivation begins to fluctuate. Understanding how a coach motivates their clients can help you understand if their approach fits with how you're motivated.

10. **Transitioning to Independence:** How do you help your clients transition from needing your support to being independent? How many clients have you successfully transitioned in this way? Can I speak with any of them as a reference?

    The person you choose must empower you to learn skills to navigate all areas of your life independently and successfully. This question will inform you of how the coach will fulfill this task.

    It will also provide you with their rate of success in transitioning and gives you individuals you can speak with who have gone through this transition with the coach.

EMOTIONAL MIND MAP

As mentioned in Chapter 4, creating a mind map to visualize your emotions can help you identify connections between your emotions and root causes. Once you can see where your emotions are triggering, you can make informed decisions around them.

You can find both an example of an emotional mind map and a blank copy to download free at silenceyourinnercritic.com.

SELF-CARE ROUTINE TEMPLATE

Along with the emotional mind map, you can find a template for creating your personalized self-care routine. There is both an example and a blank PDF template available to download at silenceyourinnercritic.com.

GUIDED MEDITATIONS

Finally, to contribute to your self-relationship journey, I've created a library of the guided meditations provided in this book at silenceyourinnercritic.com. Put your headphones on, relax, and enjoy.

ACKNOWLEDGMENTS

First and foremost, I would like to thank my amazing partner, Austin. Your contributions and feedback have made a significant impact on how this book evolved. Thank you for always seeing the vision, lovingly uniting in it, and moving toward it with fearlessness. You are one in a billion.

Heartfelt gratitude also goes out to Bob and Ellen, not only for their unwavering love and support, but also for generously providing me with a serene and conducive environment to focus and write. Your kindness and hospitality have been invaluable.

A special thanks to the Suivera team for their exceptional support. Your belief in our vision as a whole and swift involvement, utilizing your skills and expertise, have contributed to the creation of something truly magical.

Huge love and appreciation go out to my family: Josh, James, Norma, Ron, Rachel, Cailin, Kara, River, and my brother on the other side, Jimmy. The love you all have shown me throughout life serves as my North Star, always guiding me and showing me what's possible. Thank you all for being a part of my hero's journey. I love you.

Writing *Silence Your Inner Critic* has been an incredible journey, one that I could not have completed without the support and guidance of many wonderful professionals in the industry.

My deepest gratitude goes to Natalie Ehmka-Hunter, whose introduction to Morgan James Publishing was game-changing. Your belief in my work and your unwavering support have been invaluable.

To my amazing editors, Anastasia Voli and Cortney Donelson, your keen insights, meticulous attention to detail, and relentless dedication have shaped this book into what it is today. Thank you for your patience, your expertise, and for pushing me to bring out the best in my writing.

A heartfelt thank you to the publishing team at Morgan James Publishing: David Hancock, Bethany Marshall, and Emily Madison. Your vision, encouragement, and professional guidance have been instrumental in bringing this book to life. I am deeply grateful for your trust and for providing a platform to share this work with the world. I would also like to extend gratitude to the entire team at Morgan James Publishing. Your collective effort, support, and belief in this project have been the fire that kept my fire burning even in the darkest moments. It has been a privilege to work with such a talented and dedicated group of professionals.

Finally, I would like to acknowledge Robert Doran from our own Suivera team for his invaluable contributions. Your hard work behind the scenes has made this journey smoother and more enriching.

To all of you, thank you from the bottom of my heart. Your support has not only made this book possible, but has also enriched my life in countless ways.

FINAL CALL TO ACTION

While *Silence Your Inner Critic* encourages you to apply the content you learn throughout the book in real time, your Inner Champion's job is never finished. For additional support from your "gal in the chair" and my trusted Suivera Squad visit us at silenceyourinnercritic.com, where we offer resources and bonus material.

SCAN ME

ABOUT THE AUTHOR

Amber Mikesell is a leader in the field of human transformation, receiving international recognition as a Master Life Coach & Integrative Health Coach. Along with her private practice, she is the Founder and Lead Minister of Suivera, a nonprofit all-faiths organization with a mission to inspire and nurture heart-centered living across all faiths and beliefs.

As a coach and educator, Amber has traveled the world and supported over 1.2 million individuals and organizations in more than 110 countries. Her approach begins with self-love as the foundation. Her heart-centered programs empower individuals to witness how a healthy sense of self-love can heal on multiple levels—not only for the individual practicing self-love, but also for their families, social circles, and the communities they foster.

Amber's education includes a Bachelor's Degree in Communication and a Master's Degree in Quantum Sciences. In addition to her degrees, Amber has in-depth studies in world religion, world cultures, and social sciences. She holds multiple certifications in health and wellness, including Ayurveda, Traditional Chinese Medicine, multiple forms of meditation, kinesiology, traditional Vedic yoga, holistic nutrition, and plant-based nutrition, among others.

To learn more about Amber and her mission of love with her fellow team at Suivera, visit them online at www.suivera.org. To watch as she hosts *The Heart Leader Podcast*, visit www.youtube.com/@theheartleaderpodcast.

A free ebook edition is available with the purchase of this book.

To claim your free ebook edition:

1. Visit MorganJamesBOGO.com
2. Sign your name CLEARLY in the space
3. Complete the form and submit a photo of the entire copyright page
4. You or your friend can download the ebook to your preferred device

Print & Digital Together Forever.

Snap a photo

Free ebook

Read anywhere

www.ingramcontent.com/pod-product-compliance
Lightning Source LLC
Jackson TN
JSHW021950260125
77769JS00009B/6

* 9 7 8 1 6 3 6 9 8 5 5 4 1 *